MW01053807

THE BAD LIEUTENANT
PORT OF CALL: NEW ORLEANS

directed by
Werner Herzog

screenplay by
William Finkelstein

with additional scenes and
dialogue by
Werner Herzog

photography by
Lena Herzog

UNIVERSE

FOREWORD

Werner Herzog

It does not bespeak great wisdom to call the film *The Bad Lieutenant*, and I only agreed to make the film after William (Billy) Finkelstein, the screenwriter, who had seen a film of the same name from the early nineties, had given me a solemn oath that this was not a remake at all. But the film industry has its own rationale, which in this case was the speculation of starting some sort of a franchise. I have no problem with this. Nevertheless, the pedantic branch of academia, the so called "film-studies," in its attempt to do damage to cinema, will be ecstatic to find a small reference to that earlier film here and there, though it will fail to do the same damage that academia — in the name of literary theory — has done to poetry, which it has pushed to the brink of extinction. Cinema, so far, is more robust. I call upon the theoreticians of cinema to go after this one. Go for it, losers.

What the producers accepted was my suggestion to make the title more specific–Port of Call: New Orleans, and now the film's title combines both elements.

Originally, the screenplay was written with New York as a backdrop, and again the rationale of the producers set in by moving it to New Orleans, since shooting there would mean a substantial tax benefit. It was a move I immediately welcomed. In New Orleans it was not only the levees that breeched, but it was civility itself: there was a highly visible breakdown of good citizenship and order. Looting was rampant, and quite a number of policemen did not report for duty; some of them took brand new Cadillacs from their abandoned dealerships and vanished onto dry ground in neighboring states. Less fancy cars disappeared only a few days later. This collapse of morality was matched by the neglect of the government in Washington, and it is hard to figure out whether this was just a form of stupidity or outright cynicism. I am deeply grateful that the police department in New Orleans had the magnanimity and calibre to support the shooting of the film without any reservation. They know — as we all do — that the overwhelming majority of their force performed in a way that deserves nothing but admiration.

New Orleans. This was fertile ground to stage a film noir, or rather a new form of film noir where evil was not just the most natural occurrence. It was the bliss of evil which pervades everything in this film. Nicolas Cage followed me in this regard with blind faith. We had met only once at Francis Ford Coppola's, his uncle's, winery in Napa Valley almost three decades ago when Nicolas was an adolescent, and I was about to set out for the Peruvian jungle in order to move a ship over a mountain. Now, we wondered why and how we had eluded each other ever since, why we had never worked together, and it became instantly clear that we would do this film together, or neither one of us would do it. There was an urge in both of us to join forces.

Film noir always is a consequence of the Climate of Time; it needs a growing sense of insecurity, of depression. The literature of Raymond Chandler and Dashiell Hammett is a child of the Great Depression, with film noir as its sibling. I sensed something coming in the months leading up to the making of the film: a breakdown which was so obvious in New Orleans, and half a year before finances and the economy collapsed, the signs were written on the wall. Even films like *Batman* turned out to be much darker than anyone expected. What finally woke me up was a banality: when attempting to lease a car I was confronted by the dealership with the unpleasant news that my credit score was abysmal, and hence I had to pay a much higher monthly rate. Why is that, I asked — I had always paid my bills, I had never owed money to anyone. That was exactly my problem: I had never borrowed money, had hardly ever used a credit card, and my bank account was not in the red. But the system punished you for not owing money, and rewarded those who did. I realized that the entire system was sick, that this could not go well, and I instantly withdrew money I had invested in stock of Lehman Brothers while a bank manager, ecstatic, with shuddering urgency, was trying to persuade me to buy even more of it.

—

Concerning Lena Herzog's photos: there was an agreement upon Lena's request that they would not have to depict the content, the highlight of a scene, something production stills would always do. The photos would rather capture something different; they would represent the Inner Landscape of the scene, the state of introspection, moments of self reflection of the actors and actresses — in contrast to what an actor in a film has to do, a projection to the outside.

It was done like this: after a scene was finished for the film camera, the photographer would have the actors and the set for herself, and stage her own interior view of the content. Hence, many of the pictures have no outward correlation to the film itself like, for example, the image on the cover of this book. I love the fact that there is a separate reality in these photos. They speak for themselves.

As to the screenplay: it is William Finkelstein's text, but as usual during my work as a director it kept shifting, demanding its own life, and I invented new scenes such as a new beginning and a new end, the iguanas, the "dancing" soul (actually this is Finkelstein's, who plays a very convincing gangster in the film), the childhood story of pirate's treasure, and a spoon of sterling silver. I also deleted quite a number of scenes where the

protagonist takes drugs, simply because I personally dislike the culture of drugs.

Sometimes changes entered to everyone's surprise. To give one example: Nicolas knew that sometimes after a scene was shot I would not shut down the camera if I sensed there was more to it, a gesture, an odd laughter, or an "afterthought" from a man left alone with all the weight of a rolling camera, the lights, the sound recording, the expectant eyes of a crew upon him. I simply would not call "cut" and leave him exposed and suspended under the pressure of the moment.

He, the Bad Lieutenant, after restless deeds of evil, takes refuge in a cheap hotel room, and has an unexpected encounter with the former prisoner whom he had rescued from drowning in a flooded prison tract at the beginning of the film. The young man, now a waiter delivering room service, notices there is something wrong with the Lieutenant, and offers to get him out of there. I kept the camera rolling, but nothing more came from Nicolas. "What, for Heaven's sake, could I have added," he asked. And without thinking for a second I said, "Do fish have dreams?" We shot the scene once more with this line, and it looked good and strange and dark. But it required being anchored in yet an additional scene at the very end of the film, with both men, distant in dreams leaning against the glass of a huge aquarium where sharks and rays and large fish move slowly as if they indeed were caught in the dreams of a distant and incomprehensible world.

I love cinema for moments like this.

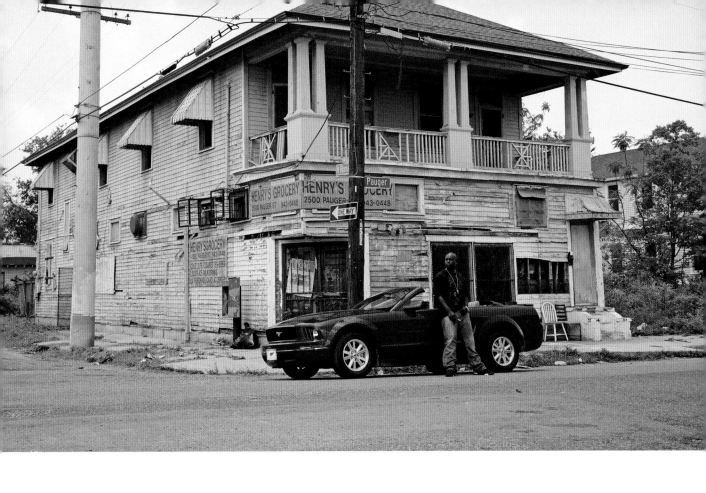

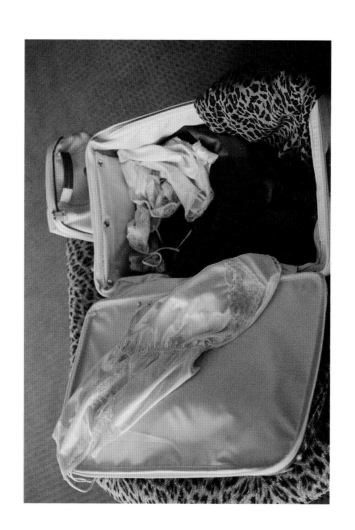

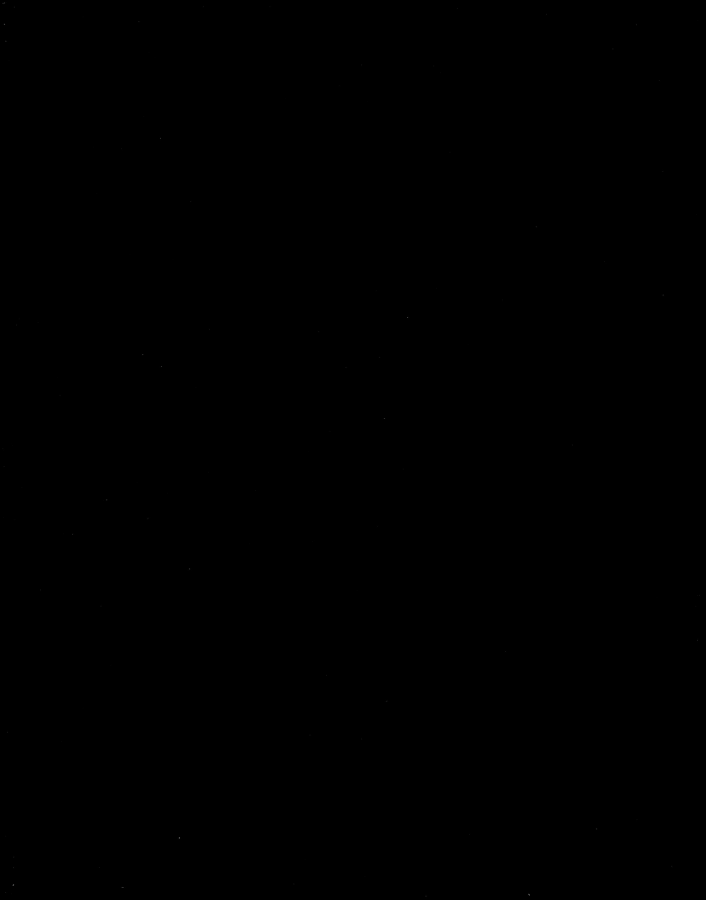

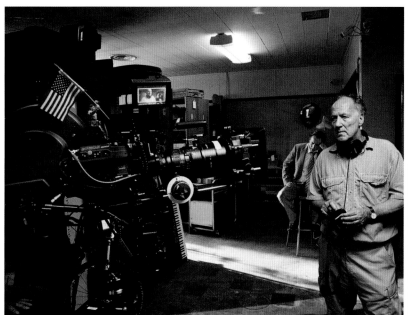

The Bad Lieutenant
Port of Call: New Orleans

by
William Finkelstein
with additional scenes and dialogue by
Werner Herzog

FADE IN:

INT. CORRIDOR - DAY

We see brackish water flooding through an interior space though we can't make out where
it is. A SNAKE moves through the water from one side of the space to the other. It stops,
its attention drawn to something. We hear a man's frightened yell. PULL BACK to reveal
the interior space to be a jail corridor. The man yelling is in a cell flooding with water.

                                                                                   CUT TO:

INT. LOCKER ROOM - DAY

The aftermath of the hurricane, the levees have broken. The room is deserted, benches
are overturned, windows broken. TERENCE McDONAGH-good-looking with off-center good
looks, still carries himself like an athlete, enters with STEVIE PRUIT-hot-tempered
detective with enough years on the job to be pissed off at everybody—

                         TERENCE
              Duffy split?

                          PRUIT
              Yeah, fucking Duffy, Cavanaugh, Tyrell.
              Duffy rolls out of here in a brand new
              Cadillac off the lot and has the nerve to
              ask me to clean out his fucking locker and
              save it for him.

                         TERENCE
              Probably has dirty pictures of his wife.

                          PRUIT
              I don't know what the fuck's in here.

PRUIT opens the locker and TERENCE begins rifling through the locker, rosary beads,
workout equipment, etc. Terence finds an envelope. He dumps it out. Sure enough—
Polaroids of Duffy's wife-a buxom skank-in various suggestive poses—

                         TERENCE
              Uh huh.

                          PRUIT
              He does have dirty pictures of his wife.

                         TERENCE
          Yes. He does.

                          PRUIT
          He met her at Hooters.

                         TERENCE
          Yep. You like that, huh.

                          PRUIT
          Mmmm.

                         TERENCE
          Alright. Here's what I am gonna do. We're
          gonna keep 'em.

                          PRUIT
          Well, now, I gotta answer to Duffy for that.

                         TERENCE
          I'll answer to him.

                          PRUIT
           Well, he's a dufus but he's not a bad guy.

                         TERENCE
          Fuck Duffy. Just fuck him. Fuck all of them.

Terence finds a stack of papers in Duffy's locker. He starts going through them—

                         TERENCE
          Five copies of an arrest report. If the
          prisoner was transported there wouldn't
          still be five copies here. Duffy might've
          left him downstairs. What's his name?
          Chavez. Let's go find him.

Terence and Pruit leave the locker room to find the prisoner.

                                                                    CUT TO:

INT. PRECINCT LOWER LEVEL - DAY

Terence and Pruit enter onto a narrow catwalk above a row of cells. The outside wall has
crumbled and water is flooding into the corridor from outside. A hoarse, panic-stricken
voice is heard—

                         CHAVEZ (O.S.)
          Who's 'at?

Terence and Pruit go down the catwalk until they're directly over a cell in which
EVARISTO CHAVEZ—twenties, junkie, thief—is up to his chin in water—

                          PRUIT
          Strange, because the manifest said the
          prisoners were all evacuated.

                         TERENCE
          Anything's possible in this storm.

                        CHAVEZ
Who's that?

                        TERENCE
Feel a bet coming on... should we open the
casino?

                        CHAVEZ
(Pleading) Please.

                        TERENCE
(looks at his watch) Alright. Up to his
nose by four o'clock.

                        CHAVEZ
What the fuck took you so long, man? Please.

                        TERENCE
Please what, shitbird?

                        CHAVEZ
Get me the fuck outta here, man. The water's
rising. It's been rising for like three
hours. It's already up to my neck. I'm not
gonna be able to fucking stand here long,
man. I'm gonna fucking drown, man. The
water doesn't stop, man. It keeps rising
and shit man. Get me the fuck outta here!
There's fucking snakes and shit in this
water, bro. Get me out.

The water's risen over his chin—

                        PRUIT
(to Terence) Twenty bucks and the Polaroids
says nothing happens before five.

                        TERENCE
Twenty bucks? What the fuck is that? Let's
make it worth our while at least—a dime.

                        PRUIT
I'm not bettin' you no thousand dollars.

                        TERENCE
Five hundred.

                        CHAVEZ
Get me the fuck outta here, man. The water
keeps rising. Man, get me the fuck outta
here.

                        PRUIT
Alright, two hundred. And the Polaroids.

                        CHAVEZ
Please, motherfuckers, please. I got a broke
leg, sir. Please get me outta here.

                        TERENCE
            Please what, shitturd?

                              CHAVEZ
          I got a broke leg, sir. Please get me outta
          here.

                              TERENCE
          Wait a minute. You want me to get wet on
          account of you?

                              PRUIT
          Think the world owes you a living, huh?

                              CHAVEZ
          I'm gonna drown, sir.

                              TERENCE
          Hey man, I got on Swiss cotton underpants.
          Yeah that's right. Cost fifty-five dollars a
          pair. You think I wanna get all this brown
          water and shit all over them? That don't
          come out.

                              PRUIT
          You got underwear on that costs fifty-five
          dollars?

                              TERENCE
          My girl give 'em to me.

Chavez starts to pray.

                              PRUIT
          (to Terence) C'mon—we'll get the time of
          death from the autopsy.

                              CHAVEZ
          En el Nombre del Padre y del Hijo y del
          Santo Espiritu

Terence looks at this junkie preparing to meet his death for a beat, and takes his
jacket off and hands it to Pruit—

                              PRUIT
          What are you doing?

                              TERENCE
          Hold this.

                              PRUIT
          Aww, come on man. Let the Fire Department
          get him out. What are you crazy? He ain't
          worth it. Come on, man. You are crazy.

Terence drops himself into the water.

                              PRUIT (O.S)
          You OK, man? You OK?

                                                              CUT TO:

INT. DOCTOR MILBURN'S OFFICE - DAY

                                                              109

DR. MILBURN—fifties, distinguished—is looking at an X-ray on a lightbox scratching his chin. He then takes it off and walks over to Terence sitting on the examining table.

> DR. MILBURN
> Well, the good news, Terence, is I'll
> okay you to return to full duty. The bad
> news is that in all likelihood you'll be
> experiencing moderate to severe back pain.

> TERENCE
> How severe?

> DR. MILBURN
> You'll want to be taking something for it. I'm
> gonna write you a prescription for Vicodin.

> TERENCE
> For how long?

> DR. MILBURN
> From now on.

> TERENCE
> No. For how long am I gonna have pain?

> DR. MILBURN
> We're gonna try to manage this as long as
> we can.

> TERENCE
> For the rest of my life?

> DR. MILBURN
> Probably. But they are making advancements
> every day, so, just work with me on this,
> alright? When this runs out, just call the
> office.

Terence takes the prescription from Dr. Milburn.

CUT TO:

INT. BANQUET HALL - DAY

Promotion ceremony in progress. The CHIEF OF POLICE is at the podium—

> CHIEF
> Thank you for helping me honor our fallen
> heroes today. We will now move on to the
> awards and promotions. Among those being
> promoted to Lieutenant today, it gives me
> great pleasure to additionally award the
> Distinguished Service Cross to Sergeant
> —now Lieutenant—Terence McDonagh, in
> recognition of extreme valor in the line
> of duty. Congratulations, Lieutenant.

To the applause and cheers of the audience, Terence—in dress uniform—walks with difficulty to be given the medal.

CUT TO:

EXT. HOUSING PROJECT - DAY

Super "SIX MONTHS LATER." Terence pulls up in an unmarked car.

CUT TO:

INT. TERENCE'S CAR - DAY

Terence wears a suit and tie. He reaches into the jacket pocket, takes out a vial of coke, dumps some out on the back of his hand, snorts it, and then checks his nose in the rear-view mirror, wiping away any excess.

CUT TO:

EXT. CRIME SCENE - DAY

Police cars, ambulances and coroners' vans parked every which way. Yellow tape blocks off a courtyard. Neighbors stand peering at the building as crime scene personnel come in and out. Terence gets out of his car, ducks under the tape, his shield now out. He enters the building.

CUT TO:

INT. CRIME SCENE APARTMENT - DAY

Terence enters a cramped apartment. An AFRICAN MAN is sitting on a chair, dead from gunshot wounds. Sprawled dead on the floor is an ELDERLY AFRICAN WOMAN. A UNIFORM SERGEANT approaches and lifts up the tarp from the dead man.

                         SERGEANT
               There's three more.

The Sergeant indicates a room inside. Terence goes in that direction, goes to the kitchen where he sees Stevie Pruit climbing over three bodies on the floor covered by a yellow tarp.

                         PRUIT
               You don't wanna look. It's execution style.

Terence leans down to lift up the tarp covering the bodies, takes a look and then gets up to walk into the adjoining room where he just came from.

                         TERENCE
               What'd you come up with?

                         MOY
               Scale in the closet, bundle of glassine
               envelopes.

                         TERENCE
               Dub been around?

                         MOY
               I thought he went away.

                         FITZSIMMON
               He's out. I saw him the other day.

                         TERENCE
               Let's get him in.

                          FITZSIMMON
          His baby mama's over by General Taylor and
          Annunciation.

                          TERENCE
          Uniform's doing the canvas?

                          MOY
          Duty Captain sent 'em out.

                          TERENCE
          Whoever they talk to I want followed up by a
          member of the squad. See to that personally,
          Armand. They pulling security cameras?

                          MOY
          Yeah.

                          TERENCE
          Every license plate in the area.

                          MOY
          Got it.

Terence walks to one of the bedrooms, where a dead body lies under a desk. His attention
is drawn away from that to a glass with water on a desktop. In it is a small fish—a beta
—very much alive and swimming, its fins wafting like silk in the water. A piece of lined
notebook paper is held down by the glass. Terence reads the child's handwriting—

          "My Friend by Babacar Ndele. My friend is a
          fish. He live in my room. His fin is a cloud.
          He see me when I sleep."

Terence takes out a handkerchief and puts it on the top edge of the glass with the fish
in it. He looks through the glass and then puts it back down on the desk.

                                                              CUT TO:

INT. SQUAD ROOM - MORNING

Terence stands near CAPTAIN JAMES BRACEY—military bearing who addresses a group of a
dozen detectives—

                          CAPTAIN
          Couple's names—Daouda and Yacine Ndele,
          Daouda's mother's name's Rainatulai Ndele,
          childrens' names—Animata and Babacar.

ANGLE ON various cops rolling their eyes at the Captain struggling to get the
pronunciations right—

                          CAPTAIN
          Family's from Senegal, immigration status,
          illegal. From what we know, Daouda had been
          dealing heroin to supplement his income as
          a peddler. Now, I want every drug dealer
          and junkie within a five mile radius hassled
          into giving up who his supplier was. Due
          to the nature of this crime you have full
          authorization for overtime if you need it.
          Lieutenant McDonagh is gonna be heading up

the investigation, so coordinate with him.
That's it. Let's see some results.

As the meeting breaks up, Captain turns to Terence.

                    CAPTAIN
          McDonagh, see you in my office for a minute?

Terence follows Captain into his office.

                                                  CUT TO:

INT. CAPTAIN'S OFFICE - DAY

Captain closes the door—

                    CAPTAIN
          You up to this?

                    TERENCE
          Why wouldn't I be?

                    CAPTAIN
          I know you're still having problems with
          your back… you're dealing with being in
          pain a lot of the time…

                    TERENCE
          I'm managing.

                    CAPTAIN
          You still taking medication for it?

                    TERENCE
          Only what the doctor prescribes.

                    CAPTAIN
          Ordinarily there'd be someone with more
          time on the job handling this kind of
          investigation. I'm going out on a limb with
          you 'cause you got good instincts and you
          don't do nothin' but work. But I find out you
          needed help and didn't ask for it, I'm gonna
          be mad.

                    TERENCE
          Yes sir.

                    CAPTAIN
          How's your old man doing?

                    TERENCE
          He's drinking himself into an early grave.

                    CAPTAIN
          Give him my best, wouldya?

                    TERENCE
          I will.

                              CAPTAIN
                    Lieutenant, no more unnecessary jumps, huh?

                              TERENCE
                    Yes, sir.

                                                                      CUT TO:

EXT. LUXURY BUILDING - DAY

A doorman building. Terence pulls up in a clearly marked towaway zone, flips his NOPD
placard on top of his dashboard, gets out, goes into the building.

                              DOORMAN
                    Morning, Mr. McDonagh.

                                                                      CUT TO:

INT. LUXURY BUILDING HALLWAY - DAY

Terence stands at the door to an apartment. FRANKIE DONNENFELD—late twenties, attractive
while not being flashy, the kind of girl who trailed adoring boys behind her in college—
Ali McGraw in *Love Story*—

                              FRANKIE
                    Hi honey.

She kisses Terence, lets him in.

                              FRANKIE
                    You bring me something?

                              TERENCE
                    You're out already?

                              FRANKIE
                    Yes.

                                                                      CUT TO:

INT. FRANKIE'S APARTMENT - DAY CONTINUOUS

Modern furniture. No personal effects, photos, etc. A great view of the city. They sit
on the couch, with the view behind them, and snort coke off his hand. She kisses him
seductively and with increasing passion. The phone rings. She lets it ring. It goes to
voice mail. A man's voice is heard over the speaker -

                              MAN (V.O.)
                    Frankie, this is Andy. Hey, hey, hey.
                    Calling to see if you have any time
                    tonight. I'm at the Montaleone...

                              TERENCE
                    You need to call him back?

                              FRANKIE
                    Nope.

Terence waits for the discomfort of her being with another man to pass. Frankie knows
what's going through his mind.

                              FRANKIE
          You know I'd rather go to the Montaleone
          with you.

                              TERENCE
          I can't afford it.

                              FRANKIE
          I can. I can afford it.

They resume kissing, and she gets on his lap.

                                                       CUT TO:

INT. DRUG STORE - EVENING

The harsh fluorescent glow found in a CVS or Rite-Aid coupled with the sound of soft-rock
playing over the sound system, the store deserted save for the lone PHARMACIST behind
the prescription counter—black woman talking on her cellphone—and Terence who's been
waiting for his prescription to be filled for a very long time when his cellphone rings—

                              TERENCE
          (into phone) Yeah... who brought him in?...
          That's who's questioning him?... I'll be there
          in ten minutes—tell him I'm on my way...
          Tell him he puts his hands on this guy he's
          gonna have a problem... I don't give a shit,
          Armand, you tell him to take a fucking break.

Terence ends the call, leans over the prescription counter—

                              TERENCE
          (to Pharmacist) Scuse me—could you tell me
          how much longer that's gonna be?

The Pharmacist continues talking on her cellphone, only vaguely indicating to Terence
that she's heard him.

                              TERENCE
          Hello, Miss? I'm a Lieutenant in the Police
          Department, I'm in the middle of a homicide
          investigation. Could I get my prescription,
          pleeaase?

                              PHARMACIST
          Do you see I'm on the phone?

She goes back to her phone call. Terence goes over the counter that separates the pharmacy
area from the rest of the store, walks back to the Pharmacist's work area—

                              PHARMACIST
          Hey, you can't come back here.

                              TERENCE
          (looking for his prescription) You got me
          waiting thirty minutes so you can make a
          damned personal phone call?

                              PHARMACIST
          (over public address system) Security.

                                                               115

                    Security to Pharmacy. Security to Pharmacy,
                    please.

                              TERENCE
                    (shows her) This is it. This is it. (talking
                    to the cop) Police emergency. This is it.

The Security Guard approaches, holding out his stick—

                              TERENCE
                    (holds up his shield) Police emergency.

                              SECURITY GUARD
                    You no cop.

                              TERENCE
                    (puts his shield in front of his face)
                    What's that look like?

                              SECURITY GUARD
                    Then why you acting all crazy for?

                              TERENCE
                    (to Pharmacist) This is, uh, twenty-three
                    dollars with my co-pay, right... (hands over
                    two twenties)... here's forty. Get everybody a
                    drink.

Terence takes his pills, walks past the cop.

                              TERENCE
                    (to the cop) Get the fuck out of my way.

                                                        CUT TO:

INT. PRECINCT OBSERVATION ROOM - EVENING

Terence enters. Present is Armand. Terence looks through the one-way glass.

On the other side is the interview room Pruit—Terence's former partner—is in with DUB
—forties, Black, ex-con—

                              PRUIT
                    Dub, look at me, OK? This is two hours
                    and that's enough. Now tell me something I
                    don't know. I don't think you're taking me
                    seriously.

                              DUB
                    Man, you gotta get me outta here.

                              PRUIT
                    Get you outta here? What are you crazy? I
                    got you on possession. You're on parole.

                              DUB
                    Maybe one, but one skinny-ass joint.

                              PRUIT
                    Yeah, well that one skinny ass joint's
                    gonna get you back in the joint. I got five

dead people, man, you understand.

> DUB
> I don't know anything about it, man.

> PRUIT
> Yambos, from the motherland. Tell me
> something.

> DUB
> What you want me to tell you, man?

> PRUIT
> I want you to tell me something I haven't
> heard. I don't want you to tell me… Look
> at me. I don't want you to tell me that you
> don't know nothing.

> DUB
> But I don't know nothing.

Pruit smacks him—

> PRUIT
> Listen, I got two dead baby yambos, you
> understand what that means? That means
> I can do whatever I want in this room.

> TERENCE
> (to Armand) You tell him what I said?

Armand nods. Terence walks out of the observation room.

CUT TO:

INT. INTERVIEW ROOM - EVENING

Terence enters. Pruit takes note of him, continues—

> PRUIT
> Two little yambos, shithead. That means
> Guantanamo Bay rule. (looking at Terence)
> You believe this motherfucker? I'm busting
> my ass for yambos and this yam won't tell
> me shit.

> TERENCE
> Detective, can I see you outside for a
> second?

Pruit, not happy for the interruption.

> PRUIT
> Uh, yeah, sure. (talking to Dub) Two
> minutes. Think about it.

Pruit exits with Terence.

CUT TO:

INT. PRECINCT CORRIDOR - CONTINUOUS

Terence walks a short distance from the room—

> PRUIT
> Uh, not a great time to take a break.

> TERENCE
> What are you doing?

> PRUIT
> He's about to go.

> TERENCE
> Bullshit, Stevie. He's scared out of his mind because you and your partner made a spectacle out of picking him up and everyone in Central City knows he's in here.

> PRUIT
> Are you trying to—

> TERENCE
> No, just shush. You think he's gonna go out on a limb you keep insulting him like that?

> PRUIT
> You trying to tell me how to do my interrogation now?

> TERENCE
> Yes, as a matter of fact. I'm gonna tell you when I think you're doing something wrong.

> PRUIT
> G'head and fuck yourself.

Pruit exits.

CUT TO:

INT. INTERVIEW ROOM - EVENING

Terence enters. Dub sits there terrified—

> TERENCE
> I'm gonna treat you respectfully, you treat me respectfully. I'm looking at some bullshit pot bust and because you're on parole you wind up back in Angola? Why would you do that?

> DUB
> I ain't the one doing it.

> TERENCE
> Who'd this African guy piss off?

> DUB
> I never said two words to him, I don't know.

> TERENCE
> But you knew he was selling dope though. C'mon.

Dub doesn't respond—

> TERENCE
> Should I just call your parole officer? He'll
> violate you and I'll stop wasting my time.

> DUB
> I knew he was selling.

> TERENCE
> Okay. Tell me where he was selling, whose
> neighborhood was it?

> DUB
> Man, look. I got me a good job with a cleaning
> service, I check in when I'm supposed to, I
> smoke a little weed but that's it.

> TERENCE
> Tell me whose neighborhood it was, Dub.

A beat—

> DUB
> Man... You know Fate?

> TERENCE
> Big Fate, yeah.

> DUB
> Ain't nothin' moves that part of town he
> ain't got a piece of it.

> TERENCE
> Where I can find him?

> DUB
> Shit. I'm saying all I gonna say. If you
> want me to lead you to him, you might as
> well lock me the fuck back up.

                                                        CUT TO:

INT. SQUAD ROOM - EVENING

Terence enters the room, deserted except for Armand—

> TERENCE
> Check Stevie's arrest report on Dub. If it
> mentions marijuana, make sure it gets lost.

> ARMAND
> What do I tell Stevie?

> TERENCE
> You can go tell him to go fuck himself. I'm
> gonna go upstairs and catch an hour in the
> crib.

Terence goes out.

INT. CRIB - NIGHT

Terence sleeps on a cot in a storage area of the precinct. MUNDT—a nervous, round-shouldered cop in his thirties—enters needing to talk to Terence but afraid to wake him. He goes back out, summons up the courage, returns, stands there until—

                         TERENCE
          (with his eyes still closed) What do you
          want, Mundt?

                         MUNDT
          Internal Affairs is checking the Property
          Room vouchers.

                         TERENCE.
          So?

                         MUNDT
          So that means they're gonna find out there's
          shit missing.

                         TERENCE
          Not if you don't tell them they won't.

                         MUNDT
          I can't do it anymore, Terence.

Terence sits ups, in obvious pain holding his back.

                         TERENCE
          Fuck.

Signals to Mundt to sit down in front of him.

                         MUNDT
          I'm really sorry, I just can't.

                         TERENCE
          Mundt—whatever drugs might've been taken
          out of the Property Room no longer have a
          voucher, y'understand? They won't turn up
          as missing 'cause there's no record of them
          being there in the first place, OK?

                         MUNDT
          They're installing cameras.

                         TERENCE
          So then you don't do anything where the
          cameras can see you.

                         MUNDT
          I can't.

                         TERENCE
          So when it was me re-doing paperwork to cover
          the cash you "misplaced," that was alright.
          That was entirely fucking reasonable.

                              MUNDT
              I'm sorry.

Mundt hurries off—

                              TERENCE
              Hey Mundt... Hey Mundt!

Now Terence is wide awake.

                                                      CUT TO:

EXT. CLUB - NIGHT

Terence waits in his unmarked car for people to come out of a fancy club.

He sees a couple—LAWRENCE and TINA—twenties, affluent, studied hip. Tina wears a
short skirt, boots and an expensive fur jacket. Terence watches them go into a parking
lot, stopping to make out and grope each other. He follows them in, beeps the siren.
Lawrence and Tina turn to him as he stops and gets out—

                              TERENCE
              Stand against the wall. Come on! Stand
              against the wall.

                              LAWRENCE
              OK. What's going on?

                              TERENCE
              You too busy making out with your girlfriend,
              you don't know when you've done something
              illegal? What are we high on tonight?

                              LAWRENCE
              Nothing.

                              TERENCE
              You pass drugs in that club?

                              LAWRENCE
              No.

                              TERENCE
              The two of you match a description—empty
              your pockets... (to Tina) dump out the handbag.

                              TINA
              Why?

                              TERENCE
              You hard of hearing? A said you match
              a description of somebody who was seen
              passing drugs.

                              TINA
              I wasn't passing drugs. What does that even
              mean?

                              TERENCE
              Empty your pockets, dump out the handbag—
              I'm not gonna tell you again.

                                                      121

Lawrence starts gingerly going through his pockets—

                         TINA
              This is bullshit.

                         LAWRENCE
              Let's just do what he says.

Terence knows that Lawrence is holding something back, puts his hand on his chest and
reaches in to his pocket himself—

                         TERENCE
              What do you got in here?

                         LAWRENCE
              Nothing.

                         TERENCE
              I'm not gonna get stuck, am I?

                         LAWRENCE
              No.

                         TERENCE
              If I get stuck I'm gonna be very fucking
              angry.

                         LAWRENCE
              You're not gonna get stuck.

                         TINA
              Where's your badge if you're a cop?

                         TERENCE
              (pulls a bag of white powder from Lawrence's
              pocket) Here's what I'm looking for... (takes
              out his shield for Tina)... and here's where it
              says I'm a cop.

                         LAWRENCE
              Sir, it's obviously just for personal use. I
              mean, I'm not a dealer.

                         TERENCE
              That's for the D.A. to decide.

                         TERENCE
              (to Tina) You gonna dump that bag or do I
              gotta do it?

Tina dumps her handbag. Terence starts sifting through—

                         LAWRENCE
              Sir, sir. Is there any way my parents don't
              have to find out about this? Can we just, uh,
              handle this. I'll go to jail on weekends, or
              something like that, if I have to do that.
              My father has a heart condition, OK? This
              would kill him. Please, let me just keep
              this from him?

                              TERENCE
                 (breaking his balls) I'd think he might
                 want to know. Yeah, I'd want to know if it
                 were my child.

Tina takes off her fur, gives it to him—

                              TINA
                 Here, this fur isn't worth much, but this
                 brooch was my grandmother's. It's worth
                 sixty thousand dollars. You can give it
                 to your girlfriend. If you don't have a
                 girlfriend, you can give it to your mother.

                              TERENCE
                 That's attempted bribery.

                              TINA
                 Excuse me? This is worth about sixty
                 thousand dollars. Doesn't that get us past
                 attempted?

Terence spots a small carved wooden box. He opens it to reveal a pink glass crack pipe—

                              TERENCE
                 Where's the rock at?

She doesn't respond—

                              TERENCE
                 C'mon, c'mon—who's got the kibble?

                              TINA
                 You want a hit?

                              TERENCE
                 Yes.

Tina reaches into a compartment in the bag, takes out a rock of cocaine, drops it in the
pipe. She fires up a lighter, takes a hit, presses her lips to Terence's, blows the crack
smoke into his mouth—

                              TERENCE
                 Again.

                              TINA
                 Yeah.

This time she puts the pipe in Terence's mouth, fires up another rock. He takes the hit,
she puts her mouth on his but this time she keeps it there—

ANGLE ON Tina unzipping Terence's fly—

                              TINA
                 This what it's gonna take?

                              TERENCE
                 Worried about your father finding out?

                              TINA
                 Nope.

She starts to jerk Terence off—

                    TERENCE
          What about your mother?

                    TINA
          I don't give a shit about either one of them.

                    TERENCE
          They beat you?

                    TINA
          No.

                    TERENCE
          Molest you?

                    TINA
          No.

                    TERENCE
          Didn't buy you new clothes for back-to-school?
          Didn't see you in the play?

Tina looks away as she continues jerking him off—

                    TERENCE
          I'm wondering what they'd say if they saw
          you now. Smoking crack... going out with no
          panties on... (lifts her skirt to reveal no
          panties)... I bet they think about you when
          you were a little girl. Wonder how it all
          happened, yeah?

A beat. Terence is nearing climax. He sees Lawrence running away and shoots his gun in
the air.

                    TERENCE
          Fucking mother fucker. You stand there and
          you watch. You watch her. You watch your
          fucking girlfriend.

Terence comes—

                                                                    CUT TO:

INT. TERENCE'S CAR—NIGHT

Terence has pulled up to a deserted spot nearby. He taps out some of the white
powder, snorts it—

                    TERENCE
          Fuck.

                                                                    CUT TO:

EXT. FRANKIE'S BUILDING - DAWN

Terence pulls up, double parks in front, goes in—

                                                                    CUT TO:

INT. FRANKIE'S BUILDING HALLWAY - DAWN

Terence knocks on Frankie's door. A beat. He knocks again—a sharp police knock.
A beat. Frankie opens the door—

                         TERENCE
              I need the coke back.

                         FRANKIE
              What happened?

A beat. Frankie steps back, inviting him in.

                                                              CUT TO:

INT. FRANKIE'S LIVING ROOM - CONTINUOUS

Frankie appears dressed in sexually revealing manner. Terence tries not to notice—

                         TERENCE
              I snorted what I thought was coke—it
              turned out to be heroin. I gotta be at work
              in an hour.

                         FRANKIE
              Oh, baby, OK. I'm not alone.

                         TERENCE
              Just get the coke and I'll get out of here.

She goes to the bedroom, and brings the coke to Terence.

                         TERENCE
              (taking the vial of coke) You didn't break
              it out for your client?

                         FRANKIE
              He brings his own.

The CLIENT—a ruddy executive in his fifties is at the door from the bedroom—

                         CLIENT
              Who are you?

                         TERENCE
              I'm the last person in the world you want me
              to be.
                         FRANKIE
              (to Terence) He's just an old friend.

                         TERENCE
              C'mon missy, we've had you under surveillance
              for weeks. (to Client) You got any illegal
              substances on you?

                         CLIENT
              Like what?

                         TERENCE
              Asshole—cooperate with me I'll let you walk
              outta here. Play games, you're coming with her.

CLIENT
I got some coke.

TERENCE
Get it.

He goes into the bedroom. Terence and Frankie exchange looks. The Client comes back, puts a vial of coke on the coffee table—

TERENCE
Get out.

The Client quickly exits. Frankie comes over, straddles Terence, kisses him lasciviously.

FRANKIE
That was fun. (Grabbing his gun) You better love me.

They laugh.

CUT TO:

EXT. CEMETERY — MORNING

An animist funeral in progress. Five coffins—two of them child-sized are lowered into graves. A small group of African immigrants is gathered. Terence stands at the back of the group. When the last of the coffins are in the ground, the group disperses. A tall African woman—MAIMOUNA—having noticed Terence, approaches him—

MAIMOUNA
Come, come. Are you a policeman?

TERENCE
Yes.

MAIMOUNA
Do you know who do this?

TERENCE
I don't know yet.

Maimouna takes photographs from her bag, thrusts them in front of Terence, goes through them—

MAIMOUNA
Look here. This dead, this wife Babacar, this little girl, pretty girl no more. He's dead, dead. All the men. My angel, she is dead. All my whole family...

TERENCE
How are you related?

MAIMOUNA
Yacine, she were my sister.

TERENCE
When was the last time you saw her?

MAIMOUNA
I see her that morning. I go by in case

                    she need anything. But that morning she
                    said she need something from the grocery
                    and she called there and had it delivered
                    by a boy to her home. Help me please. Please
                    help my family. Killer for my family,
                    please. Sir, help me. Help.

                                                              CUT TO:

INT. SUPERMARKET - DAY

A low-rent supermarket—narrow, dingy aisles, broken boxes and dented cans, mounds
of overripe fruit and endless cases of malt liquor. Terence and Armand talk to JUAN
MICHEL—the manager—

                              TERENCE
                    You the manager?

                           STORE CLERKS
                    No, sir. The manager is over there.

Terence walks over to the manager.

                              TERENCE
                    New Orleans homicide. You got people making
                    deliveries here?

                            JUAN MICHEL
                    We got different guys making deliveries.
                    Different days, different guys.

                              TERENCE
                    This would've been Tuesday.

                            JUAN MICHEL
                    Different times of day, different guys.

                              TERENCE
                    Late afternoon.

                            JUAN MICHEL
                    We don't keep track of who takes what to who...

                              TERENCE
                    There a delivery boy who hasn't shown up in
                    a while?

The look on Juan Michel's face tells us there is.

                                                              CUT TO:

INT. ASSISTED LIVING HOME HALLWAY - DAY

Terence and Armand walk down a carpeted hallway, passing old people in wheelchairs,
with walkers, with Aides helping them. He comes to a door, knocks, enters.

                                                              CUT TO:

INT. ANTOINETTE'S ROOM - DAY

Terence and Armand enter a small apartment where an old woman—ANTOINETTE—sits having

127

her hair brushed by an aide—BINNIE—sixties, Black. Antoinette has an oxygen tank by her side and a breathing tube running into her nose—

                         ARMAND
          Excuse us, hello. Police Department. We're
          looking for a Binnie Rogers?

                         BINNIE
          I'm Binnie Rogers.

                         ARMAND
          We need to talk to you for a second, Ms.
          Rogers. Do you mind stepping in the hall?

                         BINNIE
          No, I can't step into the hall. Can't you
          see this lady needs me here?

                         ARMAND
          We're looking for your grandson, Ms. Rogers.

                         BINNIE
          What are you lookin' for him for?

                         ARMAND
          Just to talk. We just want to talk to him.

                         BINNIE
          He do somethin' wrong?

                         ARMAND
          He might've been a witness to a crime.

                         BINNIE
          I don't know anything about that.

                         TERENCE
          Where can we find him?

                         ANTOINETTE
          Young man, what do you think gives you
          the right to come into my room and have a
          conversation without even acknowledging my
          presence?

                         ARMAND
          We're terribly sorry. It's very important we
          talk to this woman's grandson.

                         ANTOINETTE
          And she told you she doesn't know where he is.

                         TERENCE
          Actually she hasn't told us that.

                         BINNIE
          I don't know.

DARYL—fifteen, Black—walks in from the balcony—

                         DARYL
          It's alright, Gramma. (to Terence) What do
          you wanna know?

                         ARMAND
          Did you make a delivery Tuesday on
          Josephine and Daneel, son?

                         DARYL
          Uh huh.

                         ARMAND
          What'd you see there?

                         BINNIE
          This is a fifteen-year-old boy, sir.

                         TERENCE
          We need you to tell us what you saw, Daryl.

                         BINNIE
          He don't get involved in drugs, in gangs,
          he go to school, he hold down a job and he
          come home.

                         ARMAND
          (to Binnie) A family was murdered, ma'am.

                         BINNIE
          And I feel very bad about that but I don't
          want my grandson involved in it.

                         TERENCE
          Maybe your grandson has some feelings of
          his own.

A beat—

                         DARYL
          Well, the lady told me to set the grocery
          bags in the kitchen. As I was setting the
          grocery bags down I heard screaming. Then
          I heard gun shots. So, I hid in a closet.
          When I came out everyone was all dead.

                         TERENCE
          Did you see who shot them?

Daryl braces to tell the truth. And shakes his head.

                         TERENCE
          Is that a yes or a no?

He shakes his head to indicate no.

                                                        CUT TO:

INT. SQUAD ROOM - DAY

Captain with Terence behind him, stands before a dozen detectives. There's a blown-up mug shot
of DONALD GODCHAUX a k a BIG FATE—thirties, African-American—propped up on an easel—

                              CAPTAIN
                    This is who we're looking for. Name's Donald
                    Godchaux, street name Big Fate. You should
                    familiarize yourselves with his record
                    —goes back to '91. Did time for rape,
                    sodomy, aggravated assault, narcotics and
                    possession of automatic weapons. We believe
                    he is also behind at least three homicides
                    in addition to the Ndele family. Lieutenant,
                    you wanna show us some of those victims?

Terence props up three blown-up photographs of dead bodies—one has his throat cut, one
is bloated from being fished out of the river, one has had her head blown off—

                              CAPTAIN
                    All three were possible witnesses.

                              TERENCE
                    Godchaux has two flunkies that he the runs
                    with.

Terence reveals a blown-up mug shot of DESHAUN HACKETT—thirties, African-American—

                              TERENCE
                    Deshaun Hackett, street name Midget. Has a
                    girlfriend on Burgundy and Manzant. We'll
                    set up surveillance on the block—maybe
                    we'll get lucky and he'll turn up.

Terence reveals a blown-up mug shot of GARY JENKINS—twenties, African-American—

                              TERENCE
                    Gary Jenkins. Street name—G. His
                    grandmother lives in the Iberville
                    Projects. If he's laying low, chances are
                    that's where we'll find him.

                              CAPTAIN
                    Let's bring 'em in.

                                                                    CUT TO:

EXT. IBERVILLE STREET - DAY
EXT/INT/EXT/INT. G'S BUILDING - DAY

Three unmarked cars and a half-dozen radio cars pull up outside a tough-looking housing
project. The detectives getting out of the unmarked cars include Terence, Armand, Pruit,
Moy and Fitzsimon. Detectives and Uniforms stand waiting at G's door with guns drawn.
Terence walks up to the building.

                              TERENCE
                    (to Armand) Give me a minute.

Terence knocks on the apartment next door. A twenty-year-old Black woman holding an
infant opens the door.

                              TERENCE
                    (shows his shield) I need access to the
                    apartment next door, do you mind? (chucks
                    the infant under chin) Awww. It's OK, baby.

                              WOMAN
                    Why you need access for?

                              TERENCE
                    We had some complaints about a disturbance
                    —they're not answering the door.

The Woman shrugs, lets him in.

Terence walks through the living room to a back bedroom, opens a glass door leading to
the backyard. Just before going out sees a baggie of pot on a night table and grabs it.

Terence comes out into the backyard, goes to the backdoor of the apartment next door. He
takes lock-picking tools out of his pocket, opens the glass door, slips inside.

From inside a bathroom that opens onto the hall, G peers out toward the front door. A
police knock is heard, an elderly Black woman walks toward the door. G has an automatic
in his hand—

                              TERENCE
                    Don't fucking breathe.

G startles to see Terence standing right next to him, one hand over his gun, one hand
with a gun of his own at G's throat.

                                                                      CUT TO:

EXT. G'S APARTMENT

With the detectives and uniformed police still standing-by, the front door opens slowly.
Terence walks out with G in cuffs, triumphantly.

                              TERENCE
                    I love it. I just love it.

                                                                      CUT TO:

INT. INTERVIEW ROOM – DAY

Terence and Armand are in with G—

                                G
                    I told you everything I know.

                              ARMAND
                    This is your lucky day, son. You're the first
                    person we picked up—you're in a position to
                    help yourself.

                                G
                    Help myself do what?

                              ARMAND
                    We think you know something about this
                    family that got murdered.

                                G
                    I don't know nothin', man.

                              TERENCE
                    You were in the apartment when the Africans

                                                                            131

got shot. Who was with you? Midget? Donald?

                    G
Who?

                  ARMAND
Donald Godchaux. Big Fate. Where is he?
Where can we find him?

                    G
I don't know no Big Fate.

                  TERENCE
We find him on our own we don't need you
no more. There's gonna be five homicides to
answer for and Donald's gonna hang them on
you. That means he gets eight-to-ten and
you get natural life.

                    G
I don't know nobody name Midget, I don't
know nobody name Big Fate.

                                        CUT TO:

INT. SPORTS BAR - DAY

Terence enters, goes to where NED SCHOENHOLTZ—forties, bookie—sits in his usual spot—

                  TERENCE
Renaldo Hayes.

                   NED
Man, he's bad luck.

                  TERENCE
I keep hoping once in a while this kid'd
throw to somebody on his own team.

                   NED
I love the guy. By the end of the fucking
game I'm starting to hate him. What do you
want for the weekend?

                  TERENCE
What's the spread on Louisiana - Arkansas?

                   NED
Four.

                  TERENCE
Gimme Louisiana minus the four for a dime.

                   NED
You got it. I've got a favor to ask you.
My kid got a speeding ticket.

                  TERENCE
I'll get it taken care of, you gimme
half-a-point.

                           NED
              You're gonna grind me for helping out my
              kid?

                         TERENCE
              Grind you? You're a funny guy, you know
              that? There's guys getting half-a-point
              on the street for nothing. Grind you?

Ned nods miserably, hands over the ticket—

                           NED
              Alright. But you take care of it.

                                                        CUT TO:

EXT. HIGHWAY - DAY

An accident. A car is upside-down. An alligator is dying on the road. State Police
cars are pulled over. Flares are set up to keep the slow-moving traffic out of the lane.
Terence's car, lights flashing, drives up the shoulder, parks. Terence gets out, passes
without interest two victims lying on gurneys being wheeled to waiting ambulances,
approaches LIEUTENANT STOYER—thirties, officious.

                         TERENCE
              Hey Loo. Hey Loo.

Stoyer turns—

                         TERENCE
              I'm Lieutenant McDonagh—New Orleans
              Homicide.

                         STOYER
              What can I do for you?

                         TERENCE
              (takes summons out of his pocket) A friend
              of mine's daughter got written up for
              speeding—she was doing seventy-five on
              the way to visit her grandmother in the
              hospital. Has a couple of minor—minor
              —moving violations in the past. She's in
              danger of losing her license.

                         STOYER
              What do you want me to do?

                         TERENCE
              I want you to take care of it for me.

                         STOYER
              You come out to the scene of an accident to
              ask me that?

                         TERENCE
              We got both parts of the summons. It
              shouldn't be a problem.

                         STOYER
              Are you asking me to break the law? Is that

what you are doing here? Are you asking me
to break the law?

                    TERENCE
          I'm asking you—one cop to another—to do
          me a favor.

                    STOYER
          The answer's no.

                    TERENCE
          Just like that.

                    STOYER
          Just like that.

                    TERENCE
          Is this the same police department my
          father was in?

                    STOYER
          You'll excuse me.

                    TERENCE
          Right. Guardian of the flame, right? Fucking
          ass.

                    STOYER
          Get back in your car, Lieutenant.

                    TERENCE
          Or else what?

                    HEIDI
          (flirtatious) Hey there.

Terence turns. HEIDI BULLOCK—thirties, attractive, wearing the boots of the Highway cop
—has come up to Terence without him seeing her—

                    TERENCE
          What are you doing here?

                    STOYER
          You know the Lieutenant, Officer?

                    HEIDI
          We used to work together.

                    STOYER
          Then why don't you walk him back to his car.

Terence, not wanting to get Heidi in trouble, walks with her back toward his car.

                    HEIDI
          (sees the summons in his hand) I could've
          told you not to bother with that asshole.
          You needed a ticket fixed, why didn't you
          come to me?

                    TERENCE
          I didn't know you worked here.

                              HEIDI
              They only let me out on patrol when they're
              short-handed. Mostly they got me in the
              Property Room.

Terence gets interested—

                              TERENCE
              Property room? What are you doing tonight?

                              HEIDI
              You asking me out?

                              TERENCE
              Yes I am.

Camera pans downs, and then pan ups from the point of view of the alligator on the side
of the road.

                                                       CUT TO:

INT. HEIDI'S BEDROOM - NIGHT

Terence snorts a line of heroin off the night table, lies back on the bed. Heidi
—wearing her motorcycle boots and a bra - comes out of the bathroom, a little
unsteady from drinking, puts a boot on his leg—

                              HEIDI
              Hey. You like these boots don't you?

                              TERENCE
              You got some body on ya, y'know that?

                              HEIDI
              Yeah. You horny?

                              TERENCE
              Oh yeah.

                              HEIDI
              No you're not. You're high on dope.

                              TERENCE
              Not true. And whatever I take's prescription.
              Except for the heroin.

Terence starts to nod. Heidi stomps down on him—

                              HEIDI
              Hey, wake up, McNoddin.

Terence shakes himself awake—

                              TERENCE
              Y'know there's times I can't get what I need
              with a prescription.

                              HEIDI
              (mock pity) Really?

                         TERENCE
          Yeah, my back hurts sometimes.

                         HEIDI
          (seductive) Maybe there's something I can do
          to make that pain go away.

                         TERENCE
          You definitely can.

                         HEIDI
          What's that, baby? What do you want me to do
          for you?

                         TERENCE
          Check out your property room—see if there's
          either Oxycontin or Buprenorphene or Dilaudid
          that you can sneak outta there. Just make
          sure you get rid of the voucher copy.

Heidi stares at him in disbelief—

                         HEIDI
          You're nuts.

                                                      CUT TO:

INT. SPORTS BAR - LATE AFTERNOON

Ned is in his usual spot as Terence enters, approaches—

                         TERENCE
          The ticket's gonna be a little more
          complicated than I thought.

                         NED
          You're kidding me.

                         TERENCE
          Best thing to do is have her plead
          not-guilty—by the time the court date
          comes around I'll have talked to the cop
          who wrote her up.

                         NED
          I thought that's what you were going to do.

                         TERENCE
          I went straight to the Lieutenant, he wound
          up being a hard-on. It'll work out, it's
          just gonna take a little longer. Come on.

                         NED
          Kinda calls into question the half-a-point-
          for-nothing concept, don't you think?

                         TERENCE
          You're some cheap prick, y'know that?

                         NED
          You say you're going to do something and you

                              don't do it.

                              TERENCE
                    Good. Charge me for the half-point.

                              NED
                    And, after last weekend you're down three
                    thousand dollars. You might—you might—
                    have thought to bring me a little something.

                              TERENCE
                    Two dimes on Louisiana against Georgia.

A beat—

                              NED
                    OK. You got it.

                                                        CUT TO:

INT. BATHROOM STALL — DAY

Terence snorts up two short lines of heroin.

                                                        CUT TO:

INT. SURVEILLANCE APARTMENT — DAY

A vacant apartment that's been taken over by the cops for the purpose of keeping watch
on the building across the street. Armand, Pruit, Moy and Fitzsimon are present when
Terence enters—

                              TERENCE
                    How long's he been in there?

                              ARMAND
                    About twenty minutes.

                              TERENCE
                    Who else?

                              ARMAND
                    His girlfriend, at least one infant. That's
                    as far as we know.

                              TERENCE
                    What are these fucking iguanas doing on my
                    coffee table.

                              PRUIT
                    They ain't no iguana.

                              TERENCE
                    Yeah, they are.

                              PRUIT
                    They ain't no iguana.

                              TERENCE
                    What the fuck is that (flicking the iguana).
                    Fucking iguana.

                                                              137

                              TERENCE
                    Are we set up?

                              PRUIT
                    SWAT's around the corner.

                              TERENCE
                    No! No, SWAT. Let 'em stay there.

                              PRUIT
                    Well, the Duty Captain said he wanted us to
                    coordinate with us when we entered.

                              TERENCE
                    Is that right, Stevie? Is that what you are
                    doing now is reporting back to the fucking
                    Duty Captain?

                              PRUIT
                    I'm telling you what he said.

                              TERENCE
                    We need SWAT, we'll call 'em.

Music plays and there is close up of the iguanas.

                              TERENCE
                    Let's go.

Terence heads out followed by the four other detectives.

                                                            CUT TO:

EXT. MIDGET'S APARTMENT - DAY

Terence stands in front of the door, the four detectives set up behind him. Terence knocks
and YVONNE—late teens, Black, holding a young girl—comes to the door holding an infant.

                                                            CUT TO:

INT. MIDGET'S APARTMENT - CONTINUOUS

The cops go through the rooms to the back of the apartment. Terence comes back into the
kitchen, where Moy is with Yvonne.

                              TERENCE
                    Who else is in here?

                              YVONNE
                    (terrified) Nobody.

                              TERENCE
                    We're gonna come back every day, y'understand?
                    The more times we do, the more chances of that
                    child getting shot.

                              YVONNE
                    (points toward the back of the apartment)
                    Ain't nobody here. (whispers) He's hiding
                    back there in the armoire.

Terence and the detectives walk in the house.

                    TERENCE
          You all stay with her. Armand...

Terence and Armand go in the direction Yvonne pointed, Armand behind him. He goes into
a bedroom, stands to the side of the closet door, opens it. MIDGET—late twenties, Black,
short—is sitting on the floor.

                    TERENCE
          Get up. I said get up!

Midget comes to his feet. Terence throws him against a wall, searches him—

                    TERENCE
          Always nice to see an intact family. Father
          who honors his obligations as far as his
          children are concerned. You're here—that's
          the important thing. You might be hiding in
          an armoire but your child knows you're here.

                    MIDGET
          You trippin', man?

                    TERENCE
          Armand, give us a minute, wouldya?

                    MIDGET
          You trippin'.

                    TERENCE
          Armand, shut the door, wouldya?

                    MIDGET
          You on that shit, man.

                    TERENCE
          Shut up. (to Armand) Shut the door!

Armand goes out and closes the door. Terence walks over to the bed.

                    TERENCE
          Relax. Take a seat, come on.

A beat. Terence sits down on the bed. Midget sits on the bed.

                    TERENCE
          Now we can talk.

Terence takes out the bag of pot he took from the woman's bedroom the other day, rolls a joint—

                    TERENCE
          You don't mind if I light one up do you?

                    MIDGET
          What the fuck, man?

                    TERENCE
          I find it relaxes me.

                         MIDGET
          (nervous) What the fuck, man? Come on with
          that man, come on.

                         TERENCE
          You know we got your boy G, right?

                         MIDGET
          Man, I don't know no G.

Terence lights the joint, takes a hit.

                         TERENCE
          He knows you.

Terence passes it to Midget who doesn't know what to do—

                         TERENCE
          It's amazing how much you can get done
          when there's a simple purpose guiding you
          through life.

Terence takes the joint back, takes another hit—

                         TERENCE
          My purpose is to find out who shot up this
          apartment on Josephine. I know the guy who
          was living there was from Senegal. I know he
          was selling heroin. I know whose territory
          he was stepping on and I know who went over
          to the apartment to straighten him out. I
          found out all that out in the past few days.

Terence hands the joint back to Midget, who doesn't take it.

                         TERENCE
          Where's Big Fate, son?

                         MIDGET
          I don't know no Big Fate.

                         TERENCE
          (flicks the joint out the window) See I know
          that's not true. Because everybody who comes
          from where you come from knows who Big Fate
          is. The fact that you're lying to me about
          it tells me you're hiding something. Since
          you know my only reason for being here's to
          find out who shot up the apartment, I know
          that's what you're hiding. See, it all comes
          back to that same simple purpose.

                         MIDGET
          Man, I ain't tellin' you shit.

                                                            CUT TO:

EXT. FATHER'S HOUSE – DAY

Establish an old house on the outskirts of town. Terence pulls up.

140

GENEVIEVE—fifty, watery-eyed redhead wearing a low-cut sweater with a large can of beer in one hand, a cigarette in the other. She's crying. Terence gets out of the car, approaches—

                         TERENCE
          Hey. What's wrong?

                         GENEVIEVE
          Your father's mad at me 'cause I can't take
          care of his fucking dog.

                         TERENCE
          Why's he need you to take care of it?

                         GENEVIEVE
          'Cause he's going back into A.A. He says he
          can't deal with any more responsibilities
          besides he's gotta stop drinking. It ain't
          like I don't wanna take care of it but I leave
          at seven o'clock in the morning to go to work.

                         TERENCE
          Lemme talk to him.

                         GENEVIEVE
          I try to be a good wife to him, Terence, I do.
          But I got a limit too. He's got a drinking
          problem, he says he's got a drinking problem
          and he wants to do something about it—
          that's good. He'd been down this road before
          and it didn't take... he wants to try it again
          —good. But I say to him why don't you just
          stick to beer the way I do but he says he
          can't do that.

PAT McDONAGH—sixties, retired cop, Terence's father—opens the front door—

                         PAT
          (to Genevieve) You ready?

                         TERENCE
          Hey Pop.

                         PAT
          How you doin'.

                         GENEVIEVE
          I thought the meeting was at seven.

                         PAT
          I gotta be there early to set up chairs.

                         TERENCE
          I'll take you.

                         PAT
          She can do it.

                         TERENCE
          I came over to see you—let me take you for a
          ride, at least.

                              PAT
              (by way of accepting; to Genevieve) You'll
              feed the dog?

                           TERENCE
              I can take care of him.

                              PAT
              What are you talking about?

                           TERENCE
              Genevieve told me a little about what's
              going on—I'll take the dog off your hands
              for a while.

                              PAT
              How are you gonna take care of a dog?

                           TERENCE
              I got a friend. She just loves animals, all
              of them. Dogs too.

                              PAT
              Let's go.

Terence and Pat walk to the car to leave.

                           GENEVIEVE
              Have a good time.

                                                        CUT TO:

INT. FRANKIE'S BUILDING HALLWAY - DAY

Terence and the dog are standing there. Frankie opens the door—

                           FRANKIE
              No, no. Fuck you. Fuck you.

Terence and the dog go in.

                                                        CUT TO:

INT. FRANKIE'S LIVING ROOM - CONTINUOUS

Frankie is clearly pissed off—

                           TERENCE
              Did we not discuss this on the phone?

                           FRANKIE
              How come you only call me when you need
              something?

                           TERENCE
              You're fucked up, aren't you?

                           FRANKIE
              What? Yeah, yeah. I'm fucked up.

                           TERENCE
              What are you doing?

142

                         FRANKIE
            I'm going to work. I have to go to Biloxi
            tonight. I'm going to the hotel casino.

                         TERENCE
            How you gonna take care of the dog if
            you're fucked up and going to Biloxi?

                         FRANKIE
            The doorman is gonna walk him in the
            morning and then I get back in the
            afternoon. (to dog) Aww. He's sweet?

The dog responds affectionately—

                         FRANKIE
            What's his name?

                         TERENCE
            I don't know.

                         FRANKIE
            You don't know his name?

                         TERENCE
            I'll ask my father.

                         FRANKIE
            You are unbelievable.

                         TERENCE
            I gotta get going.

                         FRANKIE
            Unbelievable. You don't know the dog's name.
            You better be nice to me.

Terence kisses her forehead.

                         FRANKIE
            He smells. (talking to the dog) You need a
            bath.

                                                                    CUT TO:

INT. INTERVIEW ROOM – DAY

Terence and Armand are present with Midget—

                         TERENCE
            You should try to understand something—it
            doesn't matter that you were just along for
            the ride… it doesn't matter that you didn't
            actually shoot anybody. You're playing The
            Price Is Right now. If the price of Big
            Fate getting off light is helping the D.A.
            convict you and your boy G, I guarantee you
            —that's just what he's gonna do.

                         MIDGET
            Where the smoke at, man?

                              TERENCE
                    What are you talking about?

                              MIDGET
                    I might as well get fucked up I gotta
                    listen to this bullshit—so break out the
                    smoke, man.

                              ARMAND
                    You flippin' out on us here, Midget?

                              MIDGET
                    Nah man, your partner smoked a motherfuckin'
                    blunt with me before he put the cuffs on.

                              TERENCE
                    Get a load of this guy? I love this guy.
                    What are you saying. Are you saying
                    I smoked marijuana in your presence?
                    Cannabis, is that what you are saying?

                              MIDGET
                    Yeah right. Your word against mine, cuz who
                    the fuck gon' believe me, right?

Moy buzzes in on the intercom system in the room.

                              MOY
                    Lieutenant? Lieutenant, can you step out
                    for a moment?

                                                                CUT TO:

INT. SQUAD ROOM – DAY

Terence and Moy come out into the Squad Room. Standing there is Big Fate and his lawyer,
EUGENE GRATZ—fifties, white, well-dressed—

                              GRATZ
                    My name's Eugene Gratz, Lieutenant. I'm an
                    attorney, this is my client, Donald Godchaux.
                    I understand you've been looking for him.

                              GODCHAUX
                    (laughing) How can I help you?

                                                                CUT TO:

INT. A.D.A. OUTER OFFICE – DAY

Present are Terence and Captain. The door to the inner office opens and JEREMIAH
GOODHUSBAND—forties, Black—ushers Daryl out of his office—

                              GOODHUSBAND
                    I just want to talk to these guys for
                    a second—Why don't you wait in there.
                    (looking at Terence and Captain) Gentlemen.

Daryl nods, sits in another room.

144

                              SECRETRARY
                    Can I get you a glass of water?

                              DARYL
                    Um, no thanks.

Terence and Captain go into Goodhusband's offices with him.

                                                              CUT TO:

INT. GOODHUSBAND'S OFFICE — CONTINUOUS

Goodhusband closes the door—

                              GOODHUSBAND
                    I gotta turn over the names of my witnesses
                    to Godchaux's lawyer. As soon as I do that,
                    Godchaux'll look to scare the kid. He can't
                    scare him, he'll kill him.

                              TERENCE
                    He'll never get to him.

                              CAPTAIN
                    Since Godchaux turned himself in, I've
                    authorized twenty-four hour protection to
                    start immediately.

                              GOODHUSBAND
                    Just remember—we have no prints, no DNA,
                    no weapon. We lose the kid we lose the case.
                    Understood?

Terence and Captain both shrug in agreement.

                                                              CUT TO:

EXT. FRANKIE'S APARTMENT BUILDING — AFTERNOON

Daryl sits in Terence's car, parked in front of the building. We see Terence talking to
the doorman in the lobby.

                                                              CUT TO:

INT. FRANKIE'S LOBBY — AFTERNOON

The Doorman, BERNIE—fifties—holds Terence's father's dog by the leash, stands with Terence—

                              BERNIE
                    He's a nice dog, I just can't keep him.
                    She said she'd be back at one o'clock this
                    afternoon. I'm off at four and I got another
                    job I gotta be at.

                              TERENCE
                    She didn't call?

                              BERNIE
                    Nope. The night man ain't gonna wanna walk
                    it and I just can't leave the animal in her
                    apartment. It might do damage.

                              TERENCE
                How'd you get my number?

                              BERNIE
                Miss Frankie gave it to me in case of
                emergencies.

                              TERENCE
                Emergencies (nodding his head).

                                                              CUT TO:

INT. TERENCE'S CAR – AFTERNOON

Terence drives and dials his phone, Daryl sits in the passenger seat, the dog is in the back —

                              TERENCE
                This is what I'm talking about. Doesn't pick
                up the phone, isn't where she's supposed to
                be… not showing up.

                              DARYL
                So Terence, think they gonna put me on the
                witness stand by May Fifteenth?

                              TERENCE
                I don't know. Why?

                              DARYL
                That's when my mom goes before the Parole
                Board.

A beat. It registers on Terence why Daryl came forward—

                              TERENCE
                I'm sure we can get people to put in a good
                word for her.

Terence's cell phone rings—

                              TERENCE
                Hello?... Where are you?... OK, I'm about an
                hour from there. I'm on my way. Frankie—I'm
                on my way. (hangs up) Y'ever been to Biloxi?

                                                              CUT TO:

EXT. HIGHWAY – DAY

Terence's car speeds down the road to get to Biloxi.

                                                              CUT TO:

INT. TERENCE'S CAR – DAY

Daryl's asleep in the car when Terence snorts some cocaine off his hand while he's driving.
He wakes up, looks at Terence and then pretends to be asleep.

                                                              CUT TO:

EXT. BILOXI HOTEL PARKING LOT – DAY

Terence parks his car in the parking lot of the hotel.

CUT TO:

INT. BILOXI HOTEL HALLWAY - DAY

Terence and Daryl come to the room Terence is looking for. He turns to Daryl—

                    TERENCE
          You stand here—don't move. I'll be back in
          five minutes.

Terence knocks. Frankie opens the door with sunglasses on.

                    FRANKIE
          Baby.

                    TERENCE
          Hi, baby.

                    FRANKIE
          What are you doing?

                    TERENCE
          You all right?

                    FRANKIE
          Yeah.

                    TERENCE
          You OK?

Terence lifts up her sunglasses and puts them on top of her head. She has a fresh bruise
on her cheek. Terence reaches into his pocket and hands a bottle to Frankie. She takes
it, but doesn't move out of the doorway to let him in. Terence takes out his gun and
pushes through the door.

                    TERENCE
          What the fuck is going on in here?

CUT TO:

INT. BILOXI HOTEL ROOM - CONTINUOUS

Terence walks in the room with his gun drawn looking for someone. JUSTIN—white,
affluent, soft and privileged—ambles out of the bedroom—

                    JUSTIN
          Who's this?

Terence grabs him, spins him, slams him against the wall—

                    JUSTIN
          Hey hey hey hey. Take it easy.

                    FRANKIE (O.S)
          Just get my money. He never paid.

                    JUSTIN
          What are you, the jealous boyfriend?

                        TERENCE
(pats him down) Shut the fuck up.

                        FRANKIE
Just get me my money.

                        JUSTIN
I usually pay when I'm done.

                        TERENCE
Done smacking her around?

                        JUSTIN
It was erotic shit, man. I didn't hurt her.

Terence slams him against the wall—

                        TERENCE
Just like I'm not hurting you.

                        JUSTIN
(to Frankie) Did I hurt you?

                        FRANKIE
Terence, let's just go.

                        TERENCE
We don't hit women down south.

                        JUSTIN
You just made a big mistake, Terry. My
father's Andy Winnick. Y'ever hear of him?

                        TERENCE
Who?

                        JUSTIN
One of the biggest developers in the Gulf
Coast.

                        TERENCE
Congratulations.

                        JUSTIN
Tommy Leonardi's one of his best friends.

                        TERENCE
Hey, listen to me scumbag—don't try to
impress me that your father knows some
Guinea hood. What you gotta take away from
this experience is that if you ever see
that girl again, you turn and walk in the
opposite direction. I ever hear about you
so much as looking at her, you'll wish you
were born without a dick.

                        JUSTIN
Ooohh. Ooohh. Whoa whoa whoa. Terry, big
mistake. Oh yeah. Whoa whoa whoa, big
mistake. (He laughs. Starts to walk out of
the room and turns around and talking to

                        Terence) Whoa, man.

Justin exits the room, goes into the hallway, looks at Daryl waiting there—

                                   JUSTIN
                    (to Daryl) Oh yeah.

Justin exits down the hallway. Terence and Frankie come out of the room and into the
hallway—

                                   TERENCE
                    Daryl, This is Frankie. Frankie - Daryl.

                                   FRANKIE
                    Hi Daryl.

                                   DARYL
                    Hi.

                                                                        CUT TO:

INT. BILOXI HOTEL - NIGHT

Terence, Frankie and Daryl walk by the Aquarium Bar, Terence catches the sight of a
football game on one of the big screen televisions. He turns to Daryl—

                                   TERENCE
                    I gotta go talk to someone. You go ahead
                    and take Frankie to the coffee shop and you
                    stay with her. You can you do that, right?

                                   DARYL
                    Yeah.

                                   FRANKIE
                    Do you have to do that now?

                                   TERENCE
                    (to Frankie) Just... I'll be with you in a
                    minute.

                                   FRANKIE
                    (to Daryl) Let's go. Take care of me.

Frankie and Daryl walk away. Terence goes in the bar.

                                                                        CUT TO:

INT. BILOXI HOTEL AQUARIUM BAR - CONTINUOUS

Terence stares at the screen, turns to a BETTOR next to him—

                                   TERENCE
                    What'd Louisiana go off at?

                                   BETTOR
                    Three point underdogs.

                                   TERENCE
                    Three point underdogs. What are they losing
                    by?

                         BETTOR
          Eight.

                         TERENCE
          Eight? What the fuck is that?

                         BETTOR
          There's still two minutes left to play.
          (Looking at the screen) Louisiana ain't got
          its passing game, friend.

                         TERENCE
          Good point.

                         BETTOR
          Wanna hear my picks for the Pac-10?

                         TERENCE
          Do I look like I wanna hear them?

Terence leaves the bar.

                                                        CUT TO:

INT. BILOXI HOTEL COFFEE SHOP - NIGHT

Terence enters, sees Frankie sitting by herself—

                         TERENCE
          Where's the kid?

                         FRANKIE
          He went to the bathroom.

Terence bolts out.

                                                        CUT TO:

INT. BILOXI HOTEL MEN'S ROOM - NIGHT

Terence enters, checks under the stalls, exits.

                                                        CUT TO:

INT. BILOXI HOTEL CASINO - CONTINUOUS

Terence goes to a Dealer—

                         TERENCE
          Hi. Are there any other bathrooms beside
          that one?

                         DEALER
          Yeah, on the other side.

Terence walks fast across the casino to another men's room.

                                                        CUT TO:

INT. BILOXI HOTEL SECOND MEN'S ROOM - CONTINUOUS

Terence checks this men's room out, doesn't find Daryl.

                                                                    CUT TO:

INT. BILOXI HOTEL COFFEE SHOP — NIGHT

Terence enters, goes to Frankie—

                         FRANKIE
               What's going on?

                         TERENCE
               What did he say when he left?

                         FRANKIE
               He asked me if I'd be OK waiting here by
               myself. I said yeah and he said he had to
               go to the bathroom. What is going on?

                         TERENCE
               He's a witness to a homicide. To five
               homicides. (stands up) Let's go.

                         FRANKIE
               Where are we going?

                         TERENCE
               To find him.

                                                                    CUT TO:

EXT. BILOXI BUS STATION - NIGHT

Establishing. Terence's car is double-parked outside. Frankie waits in the passenger
seat, the dog is in the back seat. Terence walks around the waiting buses to check for
Daryl. He walks into one of them, hoping to find him.

                                                                    CUT TO:

INT. BILOXI BUS STATION - NIGHT

Terence scans the benches of late-night bus passengers and those with no place better to
go. No Daryl.

                                                                    CUT TO:

EXT. PROSTITUTE STROLL - NIGHT

A back street in Biloxi littered with scantily dressed street hookers and their
customers, the pimps, the look-outs, the dope peddlers and lost souls who landed here
and never left. Terence cruises slowly, Frankie next to him, the dog in the backseat.

                                                                    CUT TO:

INT. ASSISTED LIVING HOME HALLWAY - MORNING

Binnie pushes Antoinette in her wheelchair back toward her room after breakfast.

                                                                    CUT TO:

INT. ANTOINETTE'S ROOM - MORNING

Binnie enters with Antoinette. Both startle to find Terence waiting for them—

                         TERENCE
          Where is he?

                         ANTOINETTE
          Binnie, call Security.

                         TERENCE
          Nobody's calling anybody. Where's your
          grandson, Binnie?

                         BINNIE
          I don't have to tell you anything.

                         TERENCE
          Yeah you do.

                         BINNIE
          I haven't done anything... my grandson hasn't
          done anything... if he doesn't want to be a
          witness, he doesn't have to be a witness.

                         TERENCE
          This is bigger than "want to." This was a
          massacre. Children were executed.

                         BINNIE
          Maybe you should've thought of that before.

                         TERENCE
          I need to know where he is.

                         ANTOINETTE
          Young man, I would like to know the name of
          your superior.

                         TERENCE
          Right now I'm working on about an hour and
          a half sleep over the past three days and
          I'm still trying to remain courteous. I'm
          beginning to think that's getting in the
          way of my being effective.

Terence walks over to Antoinette and caresses her face. He grabs Antoinette's oxygen
line, kinks it—

                         BINNIE
          What are you doing? What are you doing?

                         TERENCE
          I want to know where Daryl is. Nobody saw
          me coming in, nobody knows I'm here. This
          old woman's gonna run out of air and you're
          gonna have a tough time convincing people
          it wasn't you who did it to her.

Antoinette starts to gasp—

                         TERENCE
          And even if you do convince them you didn't

kill her on purpose, you're still gonna
have a tough time selling them that you
took care of her worth a fuck.

                    BINNIE
(crying) Oh god...

Antoinette starts to choke. Terence slaps away Binnie hand from Antoinette's oxygen line—

                    TERENCE
Now, listen to me. Where the fuck is he?

She doesn't answer. Terence pulls out a gun and holds it to Binnie's head.

                    TERENCE
I said where the fuck is he?

                    BINNIE
He's on an aero-o-plane. Miss Antoinette
bought him a ticket and sent him to live
with her family in England.

Terence pulls the gun away from her head. Terence un-kinks the oxygen line, lets it
drop. Binnie goes to comfort Antoinette as she catches her breath.

                    TERENCE
(Talking to Antoinette) It's OK, it's OK.
That's a good girl. Suck it up, there you
go, that's it. Take it in. That's a good
girl. Good, good. Good. That's it, breathe.
(Getting suddenly angry) Maybe you should
drop you selfish cunt. Do you ever think
about your kids or your grandkids, huh?
Sucking up their inheritance through that
fucked oxygen tube. And Binnie's fucked
intensive care. You fucks, I hate you. I
hate you both. I should, I should, right
now, I should fucking kill you fucking
both. You're the fucking reason this
country's going down the drain.

Terence walks out.

                                                            CUT TO:

INT. CAPTAIN's CAR

Terence and Captain are in the car with Captain driving.

INT. ADA GOODHUSBAND'S OFFICE – DAY

Terence, Captain are outside ADA Goodhusband's office and are greeted by his secretary.

                    SECRETARY
(letting them in Goodhusband's office) Watch
out, he's not in a good mood.

                    GOODHUSBAND
Have a seat. Scotland Yard called. The kid's
in England.

                         CAPTAIN
          Make him a material witness, maybe Scotland
          Yard'll hold him.

                         GOODHUSBAND
          Can't do that. He had no involvement with
          the crime. He don't want to testify, we
          can't compel him.

                         TERENCE
          Well, we can still try flipping one of the
          three.

                         GOODHUSBAND
          Well, you can try all you want. Nobody's
          flipping on Godchaux—they're scared to death
          of him. As of now all they are is persons
          of interest—you gotta let 'em go.

                         TERENCE
          Oh come on! Five homicides and you're
          letting him go?

                         GOODHUSBAND
          You weren't supposed to let the kid out of
          your sight, Lieutenant. Now you just be
          glad he didn't turn up dead.

                         TERENCE

          This is bullshit.

                         GOODHUSBAND
          Get the hell outta here.

                         TERENCE
          Hey, lawyer, you're not the one on the street...

                         GOODHUSBAND
          Get out of my office!

                         CAPTAIN
          Come on, come on, let's go (reaching over to
          Terence pulling him out of the chair).

                                                      CUT TO:

INT. DISTRICT ATTORNEY'S OUTER OFFICE - DAY CONTINUOUS

Captain is physically restraining Terence as he takes him out of Goodhusband's office—

                         TERENCE
          (enraged) ...risking our lives on the street.
          'Cause you know what's involved right, you
          chickenshit hump?

                         CAPTAIN
          C'mon Terence, take it easy.

                         TERENCE
          Maybe if we had a prosecutor worried about
          something beside his won-lost record we'd

                                stand a fucking chance.

Terence walks out with Captain who makes sure he keeps going.

                                                                CUT TO:

INT. CAPTAIN'S CAR - DAY

Captain drives Terence who sits next to him—

                                CAPTAIN
                    What happened when you went to see the
                    grandmother?

                                TERENCE
                    I told you. She said the woman she takes
                    care of bought a plane ticket and he was
                    on his way to England to stay with her
                    relatives.

                                CAPTAIN
                    Any incident take place while you were there?

                                TERENCE
                    What kind of incident?

                                CAPTAIN
                    Any kind.

                                TERENCE
                    No.

                                CAPTAIN
                    Whatever it is you're gonna want to have
                    your story down. Public Integrity's waiting
                    for you back at the House.

                                TERENCE
                    Oh come on. They're gonna pull public
                    integrity into this? What for?

                                CAPTAIN
                    That old woman—her son's a United States
                    Congressman.

                                                                CUT TO:

INT. INTERVIEW ROOM - DAY

Present are Terence and two Public Integrity Bureau investigators—HURLEY and YASCO—

                                TERENCE
                    I asked where Daryl was, his grandmother
                    told me.

                                HURLEY
                    You didn't at any time threaten his
                    grandmother.

                                TERENCE
                    No I did not.

                    HURLEY
You didn't at any time, threaten Antoinette
Fahringer.

                    TERENCE
No I did not.

                    YASCO
Lieutenant, you should know a formal
complaint has been made, alleging you
cut off Miss Fahringer's oxygen supply.

                    TERENCE
Who's saying that—Mrs. Fahringer?

                    HURLEY
Is it true?

                    TERENCE
I think she might be suffering from a
little dementia.

                    YASCO
Lieutenant, we're asking if it's true.

                    TERENCE
Absolutely not.

                                              CUT TO:

INT. SQUAD ROOM - DAY

Terence enters and turns to a cop who is holding a prostitute.

                    TERENCE
(to the cop) You know I saw five of those
driving into work this morning. I want you
to clean it up, clean it up.

As he walks toward his desk, he finds Ned sitting there waiting for him—

                    TERENCE
Ned, excellent. You got my message. Good.
How's everything at home?

                    NED
What message?

                    TERENCE
Did you get the flowers I sent? How's Jenny?

                    NED
What the fuck are you talking about?

Terence pushes Ned to the other side of the room.

                    NED
Stop it. Cut it out.

                    TERENCE
What are you doing here?

                              NED
          What do you think?

                              TERENCE
          I don't have anything for you.

                              NED
          Then, this is a problem.

                              TERENCE
          Then it's a problem.

                              NED
          You owe me five large, Terence.

                              TERENCE
          I haven't got it.

                              NED
          Then you gotta give me something. Give me
          goods if you don't have cash. Give me a gold
          Rolex.

                              TERENCE
          Ned, please, I look like I got a gold Rolex?

                              NED
          Don't play me for a fucking stooge, Terence.

                              TERENCE
          Keep your voice down, just keep it down.

                              NED
          Don't play me for a fucking stooge.

A beat—

                              TERENCE
          Are you done?

                              NED
          You think these guys care that you're
          a cop? They will fuck you up just like
          everybody else.

                              TERENCE
          Lemme get something down on the Texas game
          —that's where the season turns around. I
          know it—

                              NED
          No. Nothing. You pay what the fuck you owe.

                              TERENCE
          (talking to the rest of the room by way of
          explanation) I'm a little late on my rent,
          is all. It's a rent dispute.

Terence turns to the CIVILIAN AIDE—a Black woman who tries to act as though she hasn't
been paying attention—

                         CIVILIAN AIDE
               Lieutenant, uh, somebody named Frankie
               called.

                                                          CUT TO:

EXT. VIEW OF THE CITY. DARK, CLOUDY SKY.

                                                          CUT TO:

INT. FRANKIE'S LIVING ROOM - DAY

Terence walks in. Frankie sits terrified on the lap of DAVE—a man practiced at
concealing the brutal part of his nature.

                         TERENCE
               What's going on?

                         DAVE
               All kinds of things. Come closer.

Terence comes into the room warily—

                         DAVE
               I'm Dave.

The camera scans the room revealing ANDY—a strapping young man with a blank stare
with a .9 MM in his hand pointing to the floor; JEFF—wider, squatter, built like a
wrestler, is holding the butt of a gun that is stuffed in the front of the pants with
one hand and a leash with the dog at the end of it in the other hand.

                         TERENCE
               Who are you?

                              ANDY
               Andy.

                         TERENCE
               Who are you?

                              JEFF
               Jeff.

                         TERENCE
               What do you want? Everything cool?

                         DAVE
               Well, what I want now is get this behind
               positioned right... (as he shifts Frankie
               on his lap)

                         FRANKIE
               He wants money.

                         TERENCE
               Who are you?

                         DAVE
               Sit down. I told you. I'm Dave. And the guy
               you robbed I know told you who he was.

                         TERENCE
          You make a date with a pretty girl, you
          gotta pay.

                         DAVE
          (moves Frankie slightly) Dear, like this.
          You want the schwantz, not the prostate.

Frankie complies more or less—

                         DAVE
          (to Terence) See, that's it. We engage with
          another human we remind ourselves that
          we're not alone. Plus, who knows—maybe we
          even learn a little something.

                         TERENCE
          How much?

                         DAVE
          You took ten off him, to make it right you
          gotta come up with fifty.

                         TERENCE
          No. That's bullshit.

                         DAVE
          Nah, it's punitive damages—what can I
          tell ya.

                         TERENCE
          I don't get it. She kept up her end of the
          bargain…

                         DAVE
          He says no.

                         FRANKIE
          He's a fucking liar. I did everything he
          asked me to do.

                         ANDY
          Which was what?

                         FRANKIE
          You want details? You sick people…

                         DAVE
          Oh listen to her stand up for herself. The
          indignation. I love it.

                         TERENCE
          (to Frankie) Where's the money?

                         FRANKIE
          In my bag.

Terence goes to a handbag, takes out the cash—

                         TERENCE
          (to Frankie) It's all here?

Frankie nods—

                          TERENCE
OK, he owed her five thousand. There's ten
and change here. Why don't I give you this
and call it a day.

                          DAVE
We could do that. Alternatively I could tell
Jeffie to shoot the dog.

                          JEFF
(putting the gun to the dog's unsuspecting
head) You want me to shoot the fucking dog?

                          DAVE
(flicks open a knife, holds it to Frankie's
face) Or put my calling card on this
gorgeous punim here…

                          TERENCE
Look, I don't give a shit about the dog but
you mark her up I'm gonna have a tough time
getting you your money.

                          DAVE
By my money you mean fifty thousand dollars.

                          TERENCE
I'll need a couple of days.

                          DAVE
And by a couple you mean two.

                          TERENCE
Yeah.

                          DAVE
Good.

Dave puts away the knife—

                          ANDY
Hey, hey…

                          DAVE
I know, relax. (to Terence) The boys want
to saddle her up. Just in the spirit of
friendliness. You mind?

                          TERENCE
Well, let her get cleaned up, put on
something hot. She looks like shit right now.

                          DAVE
Beautiful, beautiful.

                          TERENCE
(to Frankie) What are you waiting for?

Frankie slides off Dave's lap, goes into the bedroom—

                         TERENCE
          (looks at his watch; to Andy and Jeff) Now,
          I don't want to put any pressure on you
          but she has a client coming over in fifteen
          minutes. You boys can be done by then, right?

                           JEFF
          The both of us?

                           DAVE
          They'd've been done in fifteen seconds you
          hadn't mentioned it.

                         TERENCE
          My mistake.

                           DAVE
          (to Andy and Jeff) You'll hit her when we
          come back. (to Terence) Two days—same
          time, same station, yes?

                         TERENCE
          OK. You got it, baby.

                           DAVE
          Don't make me look for you, Terence.

Dave and his boys exit.

                                                            CUT TO:

INT. FRANKIE'S BATHROOM - CONTINUOUS

Frankie is putting on her make-up—

                       TERENCE (O.S)
          They're gone.

Terence walks into the bathroom.

                         TERENCE
          I'm gonna take you to my father's house.
          Buy us some time at least. Frankie, they're
          gone.

They hug.

                                                            CUT TO:

EXT. PAT'S HOUSE - LATE AFTERNOON

Terence and Pat stand on the porch. Pat smoking a cigarette—

                       TERENCE (O.S)
          I just need a place where she can stay for
          a couple of days.

                           PAT
          Well, why can't you put her up on your place?

                              TERENCE
            I can't take a chance these guys find out
            where I live, Dad. Come on.

                              PAT
            Christ, they give me the job of bringing
            cookies to a meeting, it takes me half a
            day to get it done. You want me to babysit a
            pross?

                              TERENCE
            You don't have to babysit her. She's very
            self-sufficient.

                              PAT
            Well, I'm not in any kind of shape to take
            on something like this. Look, I get home
            from one meeting, I lie on the couch and
            wait 'till it's time for the next meeting—
            that's all I can do right now.

                              TERENCE
            Well, let your wife deal with her. They'll
            get along like sisters.

                                                    CUT TO:

INT. PAT'S ENTRY WAY - LATE AFTERNOON

Genevieve holds the bag of dope she's taken out of Frankie's bag as Frankie grapples
with her to get it back—

                              GENEVIEVE
            Get away from me, you rag. My husband is
            trying to quit drinking and you bring this
            shit into our house?

                              FRANKIE
            Give it back, lady or I swear to God I will
            stab you in the heart. I will stab you in
            the heart.

Terence and Pat enter—

                              TERENCE
            (restrains Frankie) What's this?

                              GENEVIEVE
            What kind of trash you bring in here,
            Terence?

                              FRANKIE
            She was going through my bag. My personal
            shit.

                              TERENCE
            Everybody calm down.

                              GENEVIEVE
            It ain't hard enough for your father—he's
            gotta put up with narcotic drugs under his nose.

                            FRANKIE
            Oh God, come on. It can't be any worse than
            living with you shit-faced on beer all the
            time.

                            TERENCE
            Enough.

                            GENEVIEVE
            (to Terence) You tell her I'm shit-faced all
            the time?

                            TERENCE
            No.

                            FRANKIE
            Uh, it's pretty fucking obvious lady.

                            GENEVIEVE
            Yeah?

                            FRANKIE
            Yeah. Yeah.

                            GENEVIEVE
            You wanna see shit-faced, you fucking
            whore... Watch this?

Genevieve dumps out the bag of dope onto the rug. Frankie breaks free, drops down to
her knees to try to salvage it—

                            GENEVIEVE
            Come get it, come fucking get it.

                            FRANKIE
            Don't you dare!

                            PAT
            Terence, get her outta here. I can't deal
            with this shit.

A knock at the door—

                            PAT
            Great, the neighbors. (walking toward the door)

                            FRANKIE
            You're a cunt. You're a whore.

                            GENEVIEVE
            I'll fucking cut you up.

Terence goes to the door. It's the Internal Affairs investigators, Hurley and Yasco—

                            HURLEY
            We come in or you come out.

                            TERENCE
            Alright, hang on. Let's go.

Terence steps outside.

CUT TO:

EXT. PAT'S HOUSE - CONTINUOUS

Terence stands on the stoop with Hurley and Yasco, and closes the door behind him.

                    HURLEY
          Francesca Donnenfeld—you know her?

                    TERENCE
          Just cut the Junior G-Man bullshit, Yasco
          and tell me what are you here for?

                    YASCO
          I'm Yasco.

                    HURLEY
          Here's the thing, tough guy—you just keep
          fucking with the wrong people. First the old
          lady, now your prostitute friend's customer.
          The old lady you might've ridden out — she
          doesn't remember so good, the colored nurse
          she's covering for the grandson... whatever.
          But when I get a call from the Chief of D's
          office that you're shaking down your pross
          friend's customer whose father's is hung all
          the way to fucking City Hall—you're done,
          Lieutenant.

                    TERENCE
          What do you want?

                    HURLEY
          Your gun for starters.

Terence hands over his gun—

                    YASCO
          Until the outcome of the hearing, you're on
          modified duty. Better call your delegate—
          you got an asskicking coming.

                    HURLEY
          You have a good day, Lieutenant.

Hurley and Yasco walk down the stoop to their car. Terence goes back inside.

CUT TO:

INT. PAT'S FRONT HALLWAY - CONTINUOUS

Terence enters to a different scene than the one he left. Pat knows enough to know his son's in trouble. Frankie and Genevieve take their cue from Pat that now's the time for a temporary détente—

                    TERENCE
          I'm a man without a gun. That's not a man.

164

                              PAT
          Now, look, you cut the best deal you can
          and get you the hell out of the Police
          Department. Because if you stay in, it's
          gonna get worse.

                            FRANKIE
          Terry, can I talk to you for a second?

Frankie pulls Terence over to her, away from his father and Genevieve—

                            FRANKIE
          I can't stay here. I mean I didn't take this
          shit from my own mother, I'm not gonna take
          it from her.

                            TERENCE
          Hey Dad, can I get a minute alone with my
          girlfriend.

Pat takes Genevieve out of the entry hallway into another room.

                            TERENCE
          Can I just get a day or two, she's gonna
          calm down, I promise. I'm so happy you're
          here. And I got something else I want to
          show you.

                            FRANKIE
          She's really mean though.

                                                        CUT TO:

EXT. OF PAT'S HOUSE - CONTINUOUS

Terence and Frankie walk outside the house to a small cottage on the property. He opens
the door to a room strewn with knickknacks. The detritus of generations packed away
in boxes and garbage bags. Deflated basketballs, baseball bats, fishing rods with tangled
line, bits and pieces of hobbies and sports picked up as a child then put down for good.

                            TERENCE
          I spent a lot of time here when I was a boy.
          (reaching to turn on a light on the ceiling)
          That doesn't work any more. I was here alone
          a lot. This was my special place as a child.
          My castle, and I would imagine things here—
          pirates, buried treasure. My dad didn't like
          that so much but my mom, she got it. And
          uh, before she died she bought me a metal
          detector. (He pulls Frankie over to him and
          points to the window. They both look out the
          window.) Come up here, I want to show you
          something. Look at that, right out there, I
          thought that pirates came up the Mississippi
          and that they buried treasure right there
          by that tree next to the house. So I took
          the metal detector that my mom gave me and
          I went out there with it, started beeping—
          beep, beep, bbbeep—and I started digging.
          And I dug and I dug and I dug, and I found
          a sterling silver spoon and I was so

happy. I started screaming and jumping
and laughing. I went "hey man, this is
treasure." This is pirate treasure. And
I came back here one night and I hid it
somewhere. This sterling silver spoon.
I still can't find it.

                    FRANKIE
It could be anywhere.

                    TERENCE
I know it's here.

                                                          CUT TO:

EXT. PRECINCT — DAY

                                                          CUT TO:

INT. CAPTAIN'S OFFICE — DAY

Terence present with Captain—

                    CAPTAIN
          I don't know what to tell you, Terence. Not
          a lot I can do under the circumstances.

                    TERENCE
          I know.

                    CAPTAIN
          I tell you guys all the time—you cannot
          get away with that cowboy shit anymore. You
          don't listen, now this is where we're at.
          My best fucking detective and I gotta put
          him in the Property Room.

Terence works at not having his eyes light up.

                                                          CUT TO:

INT. PROPERTY ROOM - DAY

Terence studies the placement of the security camera, steps into a blind spot; looks for
a second camera, finds it then finds a place that's a blind spot for both cameras. Mundt
eyes him nervously—

                    MUNDT
          Terence, come on. I don't wanna get jammed
          up over all this. You're doing all this
          wrong shit an' I'm here an' they're gonna
          think I'm doing it too.

                    TERENCE
          So, go to the storage warehouse in
          Metairie. That way you're not here. And
          while you're there get my .44 Magnum and
          bring it to me. OK?

Mundt nods, exits past two undercover NARCOTICS DETECTIVES entering, carrying a large
evidence envelope—

                    FIRST NARCOTICS DETECTIVE
              You working here now, Lieutenant?

                              TERENCE
              Looks that way, don't it? What do you got
              there?

                    FIRST NARCOTICS DETECTIVE
              Nine, ten grams of heroin, a Glock Nine.

                              TERENCE
              Uh huh. See that scale over there? (walking
              toward the scale) It's broken (placing drugs
              on top of the scale). See? It's useless. I sent
              for a new one. As soon as it gets here, I'll
              weigh the drugs and get you your voucher. OK,
              bye, bye.

The Narcotics Detectives go off. Terence takes the heroin and the gun and moves to the
blind spot.

                                                        CUT TO:

INT. CREOLE RESTAURANT - DAY

Terence enters the crowded restaurant, scans the room until he sees Big Fate at a table
of six people, among them G and Midget. The HOST approaches—

                              HOST
              Can I help you sir?

Terence walks to where Big Fate is seated—

                              TERENCE
              Hey Big Fate—can I talk to you a minute?

                            BIG FATE
              'Scuse me?

                              TERENCE
              You mind stepping outside? I'd like to talk
              to ya'.

                            BIG FATE
              You interruptin' my meal.

Terence leans in, speaks quietly to Big Fate—

                              TERENCE
              I'm gonna pretend to be polite so you look
              like a big man in front of your friends.
              But you give m a hard time, I'll put the
              cuffs on and march you out like any other
              shitbird.

A beat—

                            BIG FATE
              (gets up) I be back.

                              MIDGET
                    Y'alright, D?

                              BIG FATE
                    Motherfucker wanna talk t'me. (to Terence)
                    Y'ain' gon' shoot me, are you motherfucker?

                              TERENCE
                    Why would I do that?

Terence and Big Fate walk out.

                                                                    CUT TO:

EXT. CREOLE RESTAURANT - DAY - CONTINUOUS

Terence and Big Fate come out of the restaurant, walk down the street—

                              TERENCE
                    I got something for you that I think you're
                    gonna like. Let's take a walk.

Terence and Big Fate walk down the street.

                              BIG FATE
                    You crazy for coming down here.

                              TERENCE
                    I'm gonna give you a chance to make some
                    money the old-fashioned way—with a cop
                    protecting you.

                              BIG FATE
                    What I need protection from?

                              TERENCE
                    Other cops.

                              BIG FATE
                    (laughs) A cop gon' protect me from cops.

                              TERENCE
                    You'll know when a supplier's under
                    surveillance… you'll know when it's safe
                    to make a pick-up, and when it's not.

                              BIG FATE
                    What I gotta give you?

                              TERENCE
                    Fifteen thousand a shipment.

Big Fate sighs.

                              TERENCE
                    Oh, I'm sorry. Am I being unfair?

                              BIG FATE
                    How I know you ain' lookin' t'set me up?

                              TERENCE
               Tomorrow I'll bring you some information—
               small shit—you decide if you want to go
               the next step.

                              BIG FATE
               What about them murders? You don't give a
               fuck about them no more?

                              TERENCE
               Look at me. Now look at you. I never did.

                                                        CUT TO:

EXT. PAT'S HOUSE — LATE AFTERNOON

Frankie waits for Terence on the steps of his father's house. Genevieve is on the porch
drinking a beer, looking out for him as well.

                                                        CUT TO:

INT. DETECTIVE'S LOCKER ROOM — MORNING

Terence approaches the Narcotics Detectives with a voucher form in hand—

                              TERENCE
               I got the weight on that dope. Finally.

                         FIRST NARCOTICS DETECTIVE
               Thanks.

                         SECOND NARCOTICS DETECTIVE
               (looking at the voucher) That's all there
               was?

                              TERENCE
               I'll double-check it if you want.

                         FIRST NARCOTICS DETECTIVE
               It don't matter—we still got enough for a
               felony.

                              TERENCE
               What do you guys got going today?

                         SECOND NARCOTICS DETECTIVE
               Buy-and-bust on Fourth and Freret on
               Andre's outfit.

                              TERENCE
               Well, happy hunting.

Terence breezily goes out.

                                                        CUT TO:

INT. ESCALADE — DAY

Terence is in the passenger seat, Big Fate in the driver's seat, Midget and G in the
backseat. Midget reads a text message on his Blackberry—

                                                               169

                         MIDGET
          Undercovers just busted one of Andre's—
          Fourth and Freret.

                         TERENCE
          Whaddya know.

                         BIG FATE
          A man of your word.

                         TERENCE
          Are you running me back to my car?

                         BIG FATE
          Yeah, I need to make a stop first. Is that
          alright?

                         TERENCE
          Yes.

                                                       CUT TO:

EXT. ABANDONED FREIGHT YARD - DAY

The Escalade turns down a private road, overgrown with weeds, goes past rusted-out
loading docks made of corrugated metal. Big Fate stops the car by what's left of a wharf
on the banks of the river, pops the trunk. Midget and G get out of the car, go around
to the trunk, take a dead body out, carry it to the river—

                         BIG FATE
          This, this is a prime piece of real estate
          right here.

                         TERENCE
          Doesn't look prime.

                         BIG FATE
          See, that's the point. Now's the time to
          get in. Two, three years from now all
          this will be riverfront Condos—marble
          floors, health spas. By that time another
          motherfucker made all the money.

                         TERENCE
          Don't be goin' legit on me now, Big.

                         BIG FATE
          Money's money. Tell you what. You be the
          front man—I be the power behind the
          throne. It's like we workin' for a greater
          good.

The body hits the water—

                         TERENCE
          Yeah, you're right. This is a good spot to
          build condominiums.

                         BIG FATE
          See? I knew I likes you, man. Come on.

They drive off in the Escalade.

                                                    CUT TO:

EXT. STREET - DAY

Big Fate drops Terence off at his car. Terence gets out, gets in his car, drives off.

                                                    CUT TO:

INT. TERENCE'S CAR - DAY

Terence turns the corner, drives past a drug corner. Among the customers is one Terence recognizes—RENALDO HAYES—running back for Louisiana. Terence stays back, watches Hayes get into his car and is about to drive off. Terence pulls up, sounds the siren on his car and gets out to walk to Renaldo.

                        TERENCE
          I'm going to ask you to step out of the
          vehicle.

                        RENALDO
          What'd I do?

                        TERENCE
          You bought dope—I watched you buy dope—
          now stand the fuck up.

Renaldo, panicked, gets out of the car. He's chiseled, muscular, considerably bigger than Terence—

                        TERENCE
          Put your hands on the car.

                        RENALDO
          I didn't buy nothin', man.

                        TERENCE
          (searching him) No? (takes a bag of pot out
          of his pocket) What's this?

                        RENALDO
          Officer, please …

                        TERENCE
          Please what?

                        RENALDO
          I don't know how that shit got in there…

                        TERENCE
          You don't?

                        RENALDO
          No sir.

                        TERENCE
          Did I put it in there?

                        RENALDO
          No sir.

                    TERENCE
Just some freak occurrence.

                    RENALDO
Yes sir.

                    TERENCE
So that's what you tell the judge then. Maybe
you'll get lucky and he'll be a football fan.

                    RENALDO
You know who I am.

                    TERENCE
Oh I know who you are.

                    RENALDO
Then why you wanna fuck my life up for? I
get suspended now, that's gonna knock me
outta the draft.

                    TERENCE
I'm sure you'll get a contract of some kind
eventually—shit, you run the forty in
what—four—three?

                    RENALDO
Why you wanna do this to me for some
motherfuckin' marijuana, man? I was gonna
buy my mamma a house.

                    TERENCE
So, you're going off as six point favorites
against Texas. Win by five or less, or you
lose altogether, and none of this ever
happened.

                    RENALDO
Sir, I can't do that.

                    TERENCE
A fumble… a missed blocking assignment—
you can absolutely do it.

                    RENALDO
Sir, please, please don't make me do it…

                    TERENCE
Listen to me, Renaldo—I dumped a lot of
money this year. On you. I got a chance
to get some of that back I want to take
advantage of it. You're gonna tell me the
integrity of the game means too much to
you? Fine. I respect that. I wouldn't dream
of trying to convince you to go against
your conscience. (takes out cuffs) So, turn
around—I'm placing you under arrest.

A beat—

                    RENALDO
You won't tell nobody? You ain't gonna tell nobody?

EXT. TERENCE'S CAR - NIGHT

Terence drives out of a gated driveway.

CUT TO:

INT. TERENCE'S CAR - NIGHT

Terence drives; Big Fate sits next to him; in the backseat are Midget and G. Big Fate takes a taste out of a big bag of dope—

                              G
          This is Taliban's shit, that's what this is.
          This is the shit Osama give them motherfuckers
          before they blow their selfs up.

                         BIG FATE
          That's money.

                         TERENCE
          Hey! 'Sup? Where's the fifteen thousand?

                         BIG FATE
          You'll get it, man. Relax with all that.

                         TERENCE
          Did I not do what I said I was going to do?

                         BIG FATE
          Yo man, relax.

Terence brings out the Glock that got vouchered in the Property Room, puts it against Big Fate's head—

                         TERENCE
          Tell me again to relax.

                         BIG FATE
          I'm not lookin' t'beat you, man.

                         TERENCE
          Where's my money?

                         BIG FATE
          I'll get your money.

                         TERENCE
          When?

                         BIG FATE
          Tomorrow.

                         TERENCE
          Where?

                         BIG FATE
          My place.

                    TERENCE
          Give me a cut of the uncut dope.

                    BIG FATE
          Look, I'm gonna pay you in money.

                    TERENCE
          This is interest.

                    MIDGET
          That's bullshit, man.

Terence cocks the gun.

                    TERENCE
          What's that, little man?

                    BIG FATE
          Look Midg, chill out. Here.

Big Fate hands Terence the dope.

                    BIG FATE
          Now put that gun away before you kill
          somebody.

Terence pulls the gun away from Big Fate's head.

                    TERENCE
          I'll kill all of you. (Smiling) Till the
          break of dawn.

They all start laughing.

                    TERENCE
          Till the break of dawn, baby.

                                                          CUT TO:

INT. SPORTS BAR - AFTERNOON

Terence enters, goes to where Ned is standing at the bar—

                    TERENCE
          S'up? S'up, s'up, s'up?

                    NED
          No, Don't talk to me about no fucking bets,
          Terence.

                    TERENCE
          What's the matter—don't you like me no
          more?

                    NED
          You don't pay your debts - I don't wanna
          know you. I can't afford it.

                    TERENCE
          (takes out the ten thousand) Ten grand. Five
          I owe, five on Louisiana, right there. S'up.

                              NED
            (takes the money) Where'd you get this?

                              TERENCE
            What are you—my priest? I got it.

                              NED
            It's a six point spread.

                              TERENCE
            No shit.

Terence goes out.

                                                      CUT TO:

INT. PAT'S LIVING ROOM

Terence enters—

                              TERENCE
                Frankie? Frankie?

Terence goes toward the guest room.

                                                      CUT TO:

INT. PAT'S GUEST ROOM – CONTINUOUS
Frankie, wearing little or no make-up, is finishing up getting ready, having put on a
modest, casual outfit. Terence enters—

                              TERENCE
                Hey, I got something for you.

Terence takes out the bag of dope—

                              FRANKIE
            I need to get my clothes.

                              TERENCE
            Yeah, don't worry about your clothes right
            now—this is un-cut dope.

                              FRANKIE
            Just a bunch of stuff from my closet and
            then from my dresser by the bed...

                              TERENCE
            ... I'm not gonna give you much until we know
            how strong it is because it's pure you know.

                              FRANKIE
            Baby, I've been talking to your father a lot
            and I think I'm gonna go to meeting with him.

                              TERENCE
            Well, does that mean you don't want any?

                              FRANKIE
            I mean of course I want some but maybe when
            I get back.

Pat walks in the room.

> PAT
> Frankie? Frankie...

Terence covers the dope before Pat comes to the doorway—

> FRANKIE
> Ready?

> PAT
> We gotta go.

> FRANKIE
> OK, alright?

Frankie kisses Terence and walks out of the room.

CUT TO:

INT. FRANKIE'S APARTMENT BUILDING

Terence goes up the elevator in Frankie's building.

CUT TO:

INT. FRANKIE'S APARTMENT

Terence grabs a bunch of clothes from Frankie's dresser, takes out a bunch of panties, camisoles, stockings. He sees a photograph underneath. He picks it up—it's of Terence in dress uniform complete with white gloves, shaking hands with the Police Chief the day of his promotion to Lieutenant. He holds the photograph, looking at himself, thinking of Frankie placing it under her things in the drawer.

CUT TO:

EXT. FRANKIE'S APARTMENT BUILDING – DAY

Terence comes out carrying the suitcase, gets into his car, drives off.

CUT TO:

EXT. STREET – DAY

Dave and his boys watching. They pull out from the curb, tail Terence at a distance.

CUT TO:

INT. BIG FATE'S OFFICE IN HIS HOUSE - NIGHT

Terence, Big Fate, Midget and G are in Big Fate's office sitting around a desk on which there's a kilo of uncut heroin. Terence sits directly across from Big Fate with his back to the door. Midget prepares a crack pipe—

> BIG FATE
> (exultant) This the way t'do business. This, this way I don' gotta be guessin' what I'm walkin' into. I got you.

Midget hands Big Fate the pipe. Big Fate takes a hit.

                        BIG FATE
             Yeah, let me hit that shit.

Terence notices that there's a double-barreled shotgun taped to the underside of the
table. It's pointed at him, Big Fate's hand inches from the trigger.

                        BIG FATE
             Yeah. (laughs)

Terence indicates he wants the pipe—

                        BIG FATE
             You hittin' this shit?

Terence sits down on the desk next to Big Fate and takes the pipe.

                        BIG FATE
             Hey, Midget, light the Caucasian's rock.

Midget lights the pipe. Terence takes a prodigious hit off the pipe—

                        BIG FATE
             You my kinda motherfucking cop, man. You a
             crazy motherfucker.

                        TERENCE
             What'd that key run you?

                        BIG FATE
             What do you care?

                        TERENCE
             I'm guessing sixty thousand.

                          G
             Pretty good guess.

                        BIG FATE
             (to G) Will you shut the fuck up.

                        TERENCE
             You owe me fifteen thousand. I'll take
             twenty-five percent of the dope. Un-cut.

                        BIG FATE
             That means you gettin' my price.

                        TERENCE
             That's one way of looking at it. The other's
             that you get to keep seventy-five percent
             and not go to prison for the rest of your
             life. (Laughs maniacally)

A beat—

                        BIG FATE
             (cutting the kilo) Yeah, alright. G'head.

                          G
             Make sure you cut that shit before you
             sell it unless you wanna kill the

                                                                    177

motherfucker who buys it.

Terence divides roughly a quarter of the key, shoves it into a plastic bag and puts it in his jacket pocket—

> TERENCE
> Did I ever tell you about Nigga Elk? Nigga Elk? I was watching the TV, the game, right. Renaldo Hayes he got tossed the ball and he was running with it and he was running, running, running. He jumped over three line backers and in mid-air he sprouted antlers, like a gazelle. (Laughs) Like an elk. (Laughs) He landed again, and he ran, ran, ran. He scored a touchdown.

> G
> That's the crack talking.

> TERENCE
> Hey, listen, I'm not worried about you so don't be concerned about me. Cuz I'm not concerned, if you're not concerned. So don't worry cuz I'm not really concerned.

> BIG FATE
> I'm worried cuz if you drop dead I'm the motherfucker they come looking for. And then I have to worry about a nigga from Africa try to move in on my shit. Now I don't want to shoot any more purple-ass niggas from Africa. Understand?

> TERENCE
> Easy, easy, easy. Cuz I'm not Eazy E.

> BIG FATE
> Fucking guy.

KIM—twenties, African-American, Big Fate's girlfriend, comes to the doorway holding a little Boy—

> KIM
> (to Big Fate) Hey, hey. I need to go to the store.

> BIG FATE
> So?

> KIM
> So I need you to watch him.

> BIG FATE
> Well, fuck no, I can't watch him.

> KIM
> Don't be yellin' there ain't nothin' t'eat then.

> BIG FATE
> Get the fuck up outta here. Get the fuck outta here.

Terence sees the young boy looking at him, transfixed by the strangeness of a white face in these surroundings. Terence is equally transfixed. Kim and the little boy exit. Terence takes the carved wooden box that he took from the couple on the street out of his pocket, opens it, takes out the pink glass crack pipe—

                    TERENCE
          Hit me again with another one of them
          rocks.

                    BIG FATE
          What the fuck's that?

Midget looks to Big Fate who nods, hands Terence a rock. Terence loads his pipe. Terence takes a hit—

                    TERENCE
          This is my lucky crack pipe.

                    BIG FATE
          You a crazy motherfucker.

                    TERENCE
          (as he exhales) You don't have a lucky crack
          pipe?
                    BIG FATE
          No, I don't have a lucky motherfuckin' crack
          pipe.

                    TERENCE
          Well, Donald, then you gotta take a hit off
          mine.

                    BIG FATE
          Why I gotta do that?

                    TERENCE
          'Cause it's lucky.

                    BIG FATE
          Lucky crack pipe. (sighs)

A beat, then Big Fate reaches for the pipe and lights it—

Terence watches as Big Fate takes a hit. From the other room Kim screams. Dave comes into the room with Andy and Jeff, both brandishing guns—

                    DAVE
          Sorry we're late, fellahs. I hope you didn't
          wait dinner.

                    BIG FATE
          Who the fuck are you?

                    DAVE
          Third-party beneficiary. Your friend here
          can fill you in on the details.

                    TERENCE
          I'm working on getting you your money, Dave.

That's what I'm doing here.

                    DAVE
(to Big Fate) I don't know about you but I
find the hardest part of collecting debts is
having to listen to the stories.

                    BIG FATE
Wait, Terence owe you some money?

                    DAVE
Fifty thousand dollars. Plus my two young
friends here were supposed to have had a
sexual experience of their choosing with an
attractive woman. Nothing. He came across
with none of it.

                    BIG FATE
Now that's wrong. That's wrong you don't do
what you say you're gonna do, Terence.

                    TERENCE
(to Dave) My end of the dope's worth a lot
more than fifty thousand—take it.

                    DAVE
Why don't I take all the dope.

                    BIG FATE
Why you gon' take what belongs to me?

                    DAVE
Well, there was a time when I wouldn't've. I
would have taken what was mine and left the
rest on the table. But see I never got rich
enough to retire. I'm stuck doing this shit.
And I'm not young anymore. So now I don't
leave nothing on the table. Pick it up.

Andy comes up to the table. The shotgun inches from his crotch, Big Fate fires, blowing
him six feet back, wrenches the shotgun free, shoots Jeff as Dave takes out his gun.
Before he can fire, Midget kills him.

A beat—

                    TERENCE
Shoot again.

                    MIDGET
What for?

                    TERENCE
His soul is still dancing. (laughs)

The camera pans to the other side of the room where the bodies lay and a breakdancer
spins around. Terence smiles.

                    TERENCE
Shoot again.

The breakdancer falls to the ground. An iguana slithers up to the dancer's lifeless body and walks by the other bodies toward the door.

                                                        CUT TO:

INT. SQUAD ROOM — NIGHT

Armand at his desk. Terence enters, approaches—

                         TERENCE
               What are you doing tonight?

                         ARMAND
               I'm getting ready to go to bed.

                         TERENCE
               Just for fun, why don't you stop by the
               apartment on Josephine.

                         ARMAND
               For fun?

                         TERENCE
               I think you might find something there.

A beat. Armand gets it—
                         ARMAND
               Like what?

                         TERENCE
               I'm thinking these bushwhackers might've
               hit a crackpipe while they were there, you
               know. The off-chance they dropped it under
               the bed where the kids were and we missed
               it, the DNA'd place them at the scene.

                         ARMAND
               You had a vision, right?

                         TERENCE
               Deoxyribonucleic acid.

Terence walks out of the room and Armand follows soon after him.

                                                        CUT TO:

EXT. PAT'S HOUSE - NIGHT

Terence walks from his car to the house carrying Frankie's suitcase.

                                                        CUT TO:

INT. PAT'S LIVING ROOM — CONTINUOUS

Terence enters with the suitcase. Genevieve is on the couch, beer in hand, watching a show on bullfighting—

                         TERENCE
               Frankie? Where's Frankie? She's not in the
               house.

                              GENEVIEVE
                    Frankie is on her way to rehab.

                              TERENCE
                    Rehab? What about her clothes.

                              GENEVIEVE
                    Someone'll bring her her clothes. Anything
                    else you want to know?

Terence mumbles, walks out of the room and takes the suitcase in toward the Guest
Bedroom.

                                                                    CUT TO:

INT. GUEST BEDROOM - CONTINUOUS

Terence is on the bed with the bag of heroin on the night table, snorts it up. He snorts
some off the table. He hears Genevieve walking up, Terence startles, tries to conceal it—

                              GENEVIEVE
                    You don't have to hide it from me.

A beat—

                              GENEVIEVE
                    We're birds of a feather. We both like our
                    poison.

                              TERENCE
                    You just drink beer I thought.

Genevieve smiles, exits.

                                                                    CUT TO:

INT. PAT'S LIVING ROOM - NIGHT

Genevieve is back on the couch watching bullfighting, Terence enters and sits down next
to her—

                              TERENCE
                    You mind if I watch the game?

                              GENEVIEVE
                    Be my guest.

Terence takes the remote, flips through the channels until he gets the Louisiana -
Texas game—

                              FIRST ANNOUNCER (V.O.)
                    Cannot believe what I am witnessing. What
                    has gotten into that team. If anyone had
                    told me that Louisiana would be up eighteen
                    points in the second quarter and driving
                    for another score I would've thought you
                    were nuts…

                              TERENCE
                    What did he say?

                    FIRST ANNOUNCER (V.O.)
          OK on second down Claude back to pass, he
          scrambles his way to another first down!

                    SECOND ANNOUNCER (V.O.)
          The rout is on.

                    FIRST ANNOUNCER
          And all this without Renaldo Hayes, don't
          forget. We still don't know the nature of
          the injury, just that he has taken himself
          out of the line up...

                    TERENCE
          I'll kill him.

                    FIRST ANNOUNCER (V.O.)
          But I'll tell you what. With Renaldo
          Hayes being out, the freshman Johnson
          has really stepped up for this football
          team.

                    SECOND ANNOUNCER (V.O)
          You're in the land of miracles, my boy.

                    FIRST ANNOUNCER (V.O.)
          You know, I'm looking right there at
          Hayes and I'll tell you what—the guy just
          does not look like a happy guy. I mean
          he's on the sidelines, he's obviously
          suffering from some sort of injury.

                                                    CUT TO:

EXT. HIGHWAY - MORNING

Terence is in his car on the highway going over the bridge, with the city passing by.

                                                    CUT TO:

INT. SQUAD ROOM — MORNING

Terence shows up for work to find Justin waiting for him—

                    JUSTIN
          Good to see you man. Listen, first off,
          this thing between us has gotten way out
          of hand, my man. Got waayy outta hand. OK?
          Those gumbas, couple of fucking assholes
          and if they disappeared 'cause of something
          you did to them, ooohh, man. I got no beef
          with you whatsoever. Everything between
          me and you is right as rain. I want you
          to know that my father got in touch with
          his guy and he told whoever it is to know
          that that complaint has been withdrawn.
          Finished. Oh yeah. Okay?

                    TERENCE
          Okay.

                         JUSTIN
          Oh yeah?

                         TERENCE
          Uh, phew.

A beat—

                         TERENCE
          (Points to the door) That's the way out.

                         JUSTIN
          Oh yeah.

Justin, nervous and anxious to get out of there leaves. He passes Ned entering—

                         TERENCE
          Oh nah, look Ned, if you called first, I
          would've saved you the trip. I don't have
          the money.

                         NED
          I'm guessing you didn't see the game.

Ned pulls out an envelope filled with cash and shows the money to Terence.

                         TERENCE
          How did this happen?

                         NED
          Louisiana by three.

                         TERENCE
          Hayes ended up playing?

                         NED
          Nope.

                         TERENCE
          (to himself) It worked out anyway.

                         NED
          What are you talking about?

                         TERENCE
          Nothing.

                         NED
          Oh and my daughter's tickets, speeding
          tickets? Thank you, thank you, thank you.
          This female highway patrol officer calls
          up and says they're taken care of. (hands
          Terence a bulky envelope) It's ten thousand
          dollars—sure you don't wanna count it?

                         TERENCE
          I trust you.

                         NED
          Alright, man you take care of yourself.

                              TERENCE
                    Alright.

                                                            CUT TO:

Ned exits. Captain comes out of his office carrying the pink glass crack pipe in a clear
plastic evidence bag—

                              CAPTAIN
                    Great news.

                              TERENCE
                    What?

                              CAPTAIN
                    Armand came up with this at the crime scene
                    on Josephine.

                              ARMAND
                    I just got lucky.

Terence takes the bag.

                              CAPTAIN
                    Lab found Godchaux's DNA on it. (they all
                    laugh) Yes!

                              TERENCE
                    (looking at the bag) Ahh, look at that.

                                                            CUT TO:

INT. PAT'S HOUSE DAWN

Frankie is in bed and Terence sits down beside her, pulling out a spoon.

                              TERENCE
                    I found the spoon.

Frankie sits up.

                              TERENCE
                    It's not silver, a little rusty. I wanna
                    give it you. It's yours.

                              FRANKIE
                    It's for me?

Terence hands it to her.

                              FRANKIE
                    That's so sweet.

She looks at it intently.

                              FRANKIE
                    It's beautiful. (leaning over to kiss him)

                                                            CUT TO:

INT. BIG FATE'S HOUSE — DAY

Present is Big Fate sitting on the edge of his desk, talking on the cell phone when Terence and other officers burst in with guns drawn.

                    BIG FATE
          (to the person on the phone) Eight. I need
          eight of 'em. It's going down baby. I got
          some help.

                    TERENCE
          Police Department. Stand up and put your
          hands up where we can see them.

                    BIG FATE
          What the fuck's this?

                    TERENCE
          Get up!

Pruit enters, gun drawn, as Terence pats Big Fate down—

                    PRUIT
          We got it. Check the outside, check the
          backyard, check the upstairs, check his
          car. We got this. It's OK. We're good.

Terence frisks Big Fate and pulls a gun out of his pants and throws it to Pruit.

                    TERENCE
          (to Pruit) Cuff him.

                    PRUIT
          No. No.

                    TERENCE
          What do you mean "no"?

                    PRUIT
          Here's what happens. Before we can cuff
          him, he goes for this weapon. We shoot this
          prick and steal his shit.

                    BIG FATE
          Terence, what are we doing? I thought we
          had our thing going.

                    PRUIT
          You're wrong baby. He acts like he likes you
          but he likes to get high, huh? That don't
          mean he stopping being the po-lice.

                    TERENCE
          Cuff him, Stevie.

                    PRUIT
          No. Why—you draw the line at murder?
          Murder is where it gets interesting, murder
          is where it gets fun.

                    TERENCE
          I said cuff him, Stevie.

                              BIG FATE
                    This about money? You want money? You want
                    my fucking money? You want my fucking
                    money? Take my money. But you don' gotta
                    kill me for this shit…

                              PRUIT
                    Go for it, son. Go for it. Go for it. Go for
                    it.

Pruit puts the gun on the desk. Terence steps between Big Fate and the gun—

                              TERENCE
                    Next time.

Terence takes Big Fate out past a crest-fallen Pruit.

                              TERENCE
                    Now fucking cuff him. I said cuff the
                    motherfucker, Stevie.

Pruit cuffs him.

                                                              TIME CUT TO:

INT. BANQUET HALL – AFTERNOON

Super "One Year Later". Terence, wearing full dress uniform with white gloves, sits on
the stage together with others being promoted. The place is filled, tables set for dinner,
the Chief of Police at the podium—

                              CHIEF
                    Ladies and gentleman, it is an honor to
                    conclude this year on a very positive
                    note. In recognition of his leadership and
                    tenacity in the investigation of the Ndele
                    family murders, resulting in the successful
                    apprehension and prosecution of the
                    three individuals responsible, I'm proud
                    to include Lieutenant Terence McDonagh
                    among those being promoted to the rank of
                    Captain. Captain McDonagh?

Terence walks to the podium. The Chief shakes his hand as flashbulbs go off and the
audience cheers. Terence looks out into the seats, makes eye contact with Frankie,
demure, beautiful and pregnant. He winks at her, she winks back. Seated next to her
are Pat and Genevieve—both clear-eyed and beaming.

                                                                  CUT TO:

INT. BANQUET HALL – EVENING

Terence, Frankie, Pat and Genevieve are seated at a table. The WAITER leans in to
Terence—

                              WAITER
                    Excuse me, would you care for some wine?

                              TERENCE
                    No thank you. We're all going to stick with
                    our sparkling water.

Terence takes in the others with a look that while stopping short of self-congratulation, has an acknowledgment of shared sobriety—

                         FRANKIE
             (toasting Terence) I would like to make a
             toast to the new Captain.

                         TERENCE
             To a new life.

They all clink their glasses.

                         GENEVIEVE
             I'm probably going to start to cry right
             now.

                         FRANKIE
             Ohh. That's OK.

                         GENEVIEVE
             (holding up her glass) To my new family.

                         PAT
             God bless.

                         TERENCE
             Here, here.

                                                            CUT TO:

EXT. TERENCE FRANKIE'S HOUSE – SUNSET

A pleasant house on a shady street in a nice, if modest section. Terence pulls up, and gets out walking to the other side of the car to let Frankie out. They begin to walk up the pathway in the front of the house.

                         FRANKIE
             You still gonna be working the nightshift
             when I get closer to the due date?

                         TERENCE
             I'll make sure I'm not, how's that?

                         FRANKIE
             I mean, I can get to the hospital and all
             but I like having you home at night.

                         TERENCE
             I like it better that way too.

They kiss and she walks into the house. He walks to the car and gets in. Terence drives off.

                                                            CUT TO:

EXT. CLUB – NIGHT

A COUPLE in their twenties comes out of the same club as before, head for the parking lot. The GIRL wears a short skirt. The BOY says something that makes her laugh. They walk to his car and search for the keys, still flirting.

WIDEN TO show Terence—now in his suit—following them into the parking lot, getting out of his car—

                    TERENCE
          Stand against the wall.

                    BOY
          What'd we do?

                    TERENCE
          Hey, stand against the wall! (pushing him
          into the wall)

                    GIRL
          What are you doing?

                    TERENCE
          The two of you match a description.
          Somebody was seen passing drugs in the
          club.

                    GIRL
          Sir…

                    TERENCE
          Don't say anything—do exactly what I tell
          you to do. So, what are we high on tonight.

The Boy complies, nervously puts his hands against the wall—

                    TERENCE
          So—what are we high on tonight?

                    BOY
          Nuthin.

                    GIRL
          We didn't…

                    TERENCE
          Empty your pockets, dump out the hand bag.

                                                            CUT TO:

INT. LAFAYETTE HOTEL ROOM – DAY

Terence lays out a line of dope. As he does, a knock at the door followed by someone coming in…

                    CHAVEZ
          Room service.

                    TERENCE
          I didn't order any room service. (not even
          looking up)

                    CHAVEZ
          They must've made a mistake, again.
          (recognizes him) Holy shit.

                              CHAVEZ
          I'm Evaristo Chavez, man. You saved my life.
          I was in the prison that was flooding, man.

                              TERENCE
          Oh yeah.

                              CHAVEZ
          Do you remember me? Are you still with the
          Police Department?

                              TERENCE
          Port of Call, still New Orleans.

                              CHAVEZ
          OK.

                              TERENCE
          What happened with you?

                              CHAVEZ
          The judge remanded me to a drug treatment
          program… November Fourteenth I have a year
          clean.

                              TERENCE
          Congratulations.

Terence looks over at the night table and the massive line.

                              CHAVEZ
          Are you all right?

                              TERENCE
          Sometimes I have bad days.

                              CHAVEZ
          Listen, you saved my life. I'm almost done
          working. I'm gonna get you outta here, OK.
          OK?

                              TERENCE
          Do fish have dreams?

                                                              CUT TO:

INT. AQUARIUM – DAY

Terence and Chavez sit in front of a massive tank of fish—

                              TERENCE
               You know, Chavez, I still hate that I
               ruined my underwear for you.

Terence and Chavez are staring into nowhere when a smile comes across Terence's face.
He laughs.

FADE OUT.

ACKNOWLEDGMENTS

Thanks above all to Paul Olinde for working with me
patiently on lighting and Batou Chandler for helping
find the most extraordinary side of New Orleans.

My deepest thanks to Werner Herzog, William Finkelstein,
Peter Zeitlinger, Erik Soellner, Nicolas Cage, Eva Mendes,
Jennifer Coolidge, and the cast and crew of the film.

Also, appreciation to Avi Lerner, Elliot Rosenblatt,
Alan and Gabe Polsky, and Cathy Gesualdo and the
production team of The Bad Lieutenant.

Lena Herzog

First published in the United States in 2009 by
Universe Publishing, a division of
Rizzoli International Publications, Inc.
300 Park Avenue South
New York, NY 10010
www.rizzoliusa.com

2009 2010 2011 2012 / 10 9 8 7 6 5 4 3 2 1

ISBN 13: 978-0-7893-2013-1

Library of Congress Control Number: 2009931149

Designed by Roanne Adams

Printed in China